A Little Book of Rest

Walking Out of Anxiety and Fear

Sheila Jacobs

First published 2022 by Malcolm Down Publishing Ltd.
www.malcolmdown.co.uk

25 24 23 22   7 6 5 4 3 2 1

British Library Cataloguing in Publication Data
A catalogue record for this book is available from the British Library.

ISBN 978-1-915046-03-1

Cover design by Esther Kotecha
Art direction by Sarah Grace

Printed in the UK

Dedication

For the glory of God
Soli Deo gloria

For my dad,
Keith
And in memory of my mum,
Mary

For Pam, Helen, Brenda, Maria, Jean, Emily,
Shirley and Ken

And thanks to Val and Ray, whose stress-busting coffee and waffles
really helped

Contents

Introduction

When I was about ten, we lived in a cinema.

My dad was the manager, so he and Mum and I lived in dressing rooms which were converted into a flat.

We entered by a stage exit door. From there, we went up a flight of stairs to the bathroom and my parents' bedroom, up another flight to my bedroom, another set of stairs to the lounge and the kitchen, and yet another to the spare room. And the *dark room*.

The dark room wasn't a place where they had a camera. This was an unconverted room that my dad told me years later was also called 'the void'.

It was open to the roof, with one or two patches of light as the sky peeked in through broken slates; I only looked in once that I can remember, when my dad opened the door. All I could see was a dark, empty, frightening space. It instilled a sense of dread in me. Perhaps it was the unnerving sense of a room that should have been clean and bright and lived in, but was dark and broken and unredeemed.

Sometimes we don't really know why we're fearful. It might be that we are generally anxious people. We tend to worry about everything. Of course, some fear can be quite legitimate. But if we find we're overanxious and it's affecting our lives – that can become a problem.

This isn't a book which analyses the nature of anxiety. It's a book which I hope will facilitate an encounter with the Prince of Peace, in whom there is no fear. This is a little book of rest. The rest that Jesus has bought for us.

Here I share some of my own story. I became ill in my early thirties with Ménière's disease – although I was later told I had it only mildly. However, by that time it had virtually destroyed my life: not through the effects of what can be a severely life-limiting illness, but through anxiety.

I was uncomfortable outside the confines of my own home, or town, even when my physical health had radically improved. I simply couldn't live a normal life, and this went on for years.

In the end, I became desperate. I realised how much of a prison I was in. The biggest problem for me was an inability to truly walk in forgiveness, and trust, and this seemed to be causing quite a barrier to freedom. Forgiveness, a letting go of past hurts, opened the door for a bigger experience of God, and consequently release from the kind of fear that prevented me from even going to church, because I knew I'd have a panic attack. In short, I forgave, and then I began to know a new level of freedom.

But it's been a journey. There have been setbacks. I often stumble into the thorn bushes of anxiety, before bleating like a sheep for the Shepherd to come and untangle me. It's a process, and thankfully, God is patient with me, as he is with us all. The closer I get to him, the more I see there is no need to fear, because he really does go before me, like the pillar of cloud by day and fire by night that guided God's people of long ago (Exodus 13:21). He's the same God. And I have found him to be faithful. It's a two-way relationship; me and him. When I'm weak, he's strong (see 2 Corinthians 12:9-11).

Whatever your fear, whatever your circumstances, even if you feel shattered, like a broken mirror, you are not alone. You don't have to fear 'the void' – whatever that 'void' is for you. We don't have to live in that scary space – frightened of 'whatever it is' that lies in the darkness beyond.

How to use this book

The five weeks in this material have different themes which should be fairly self-explanatory:

You don't have to read them as 'weeks'; you can dip in and choose what to look at and when. There are five days within each week, plus an exercise for the weekend.

It's a gentle journey. You may not take the same route as everyone else. Each reader will find different things that resonate and help.

It's a good idea to keep a journal throughout this book, but if that's not your thing, it's OK. Writing or other creative exercises are encouraged here, but they're not mandatory!

So enjoy – take a meander, like a walk in a quiet meadow beside a stream. Let the stress and anxiety roll away as you get closer to the One who loves you best.

Week 1: Running Away

1

1 Kings 19:2-3a

So Jezebel sent a messenger to Elijah to say, 'May the gods deal with me, be it ever so severely, if by this time tomorrow I do not make your life like that of one of them.' Elijah was afraid and ran for his life.

He's the hero! He had seen God do amazing things (see 1 Kings 18); he knew his God was powerful. You'd have thought the prophet Elijah could never be intimidated by anyone or anything. He'd just have to call down fire from above, right, and take out his enemies? Well – apparently not.

Queen Jezebel had a lot of influence. She was a strong queen, with a weak king. And now she was threatening Elijah because she really didn't like the way he'd behaved. She seemed to have no fear of God; I wonder if she thought Elijah had rid the land of the pagan prophets by a magic trick of some sort? She certainly wasn't looking at the power behind the man. But then, neither was he. Because when she threatened him, he didn't stand up and act in faith. He acted in complete fear. He ran away.

It's so easy to run when we're faced with something we can't deal with. When anxieties overwhelm us, we just want to escape, under the duvet – anywhere, really.

I went to eight different schools, growing up, because my dad's job meant that we as a family often had to change location. Each move meant a different school, of course, which was fun to start off with. When you're moving on all the time, you can leave your troubles behind – can't you?

I became used to getting out of things I didn't want to do. I'd always find a way to not face up to things that scared me. For example, I didn't like swimming, so I'd feign illness. I used the same tactic to get out of other lessons I didn't want to do. Trouble was, I missed so much schooling that I fell behind in the lessons and it was impossible to catch up. The anxiety around this made me miss more school with illnesses real and imagined. By the time I was a young teen, at a very academic school where I was failing badly, I was being prescribed tablets to stop me feeling sick before classes.

One thing that was good about school, though, was that I, along with the other pupils, had been given a little New Testament. I'd begun to read it, even though it was written in what seemed to be Shakespearean English. I didn't know Jesus, but I'd heard about him from my granny, who was a Christian, and some of what I was reading seemed to speak to me. 'God,' I said. 'I need help.' And then I heard we were moving again. A fresh start!

My new school was more easy-going than the last, and I made good friends. I still got out of stuff I didn't want to do, but something within me had shifted. I knew God was real. I was an anxious kid, but I'd realised that however much life seemed to threaten me, and my natural instinct was to run away – there was Someone to run to.

The trouble is, however much we try to run from our anxieties, and may well escape the immediate issues by doing so, running doesn't always solve the underlying problem. If we cope with life by running away, it'll become an entrenched solution. Eventually we could find we just run from anything and everything, rather than facing up to life!

Reflection

- Are you an 'anxious person'?
- What triggers your anxiety?
- When you are afraid, what's your typical coping mechanism?

Stand by for action!

If you are not someone who journals, buy an exercise book, or start a new file on your electronic device: My Journey.

Think about ways you have coped with anxious situations in the past. Do you try to flee, like Elijah? What has been the result? Write this down.

Now start a new page: My Journey with God.

Do you have a journey with God? Where has he come through for you, in the past? If you don't have a backstory with him, write your thoughts about this, or leave the page blank for now.

Conclusion

Knowing God is real, and remembering what he has done for us, can be a great help when we're going through 'stuff' today. Can you think of one thing to thank God for right now? Psalm 103:2 tells us: 'Praise the LORD, my soul, and forget not all his benefits'.

Lord, I want to thank you for … [name the 'benefits' from the past, and the 'benefits' from today]. Lord, help me to trust that you're really there, and you really do hear me, even when I want to run away and hide. Amen.

2

1 Kings 19:4-5a

... he himself went a day's journey into the wilderness. He came to a broom bush, sat down under it and prayed that he might die. 'I have had enough, LORD,' he said. 'Take my life; I am no better than my ancestors.' Then he lay down under the bush and fell asleep.

When worry overwhelms us, it can give us a sense of real hopelessness. Rather than face whatever it is that worries us, we may try to run from it. Alternatively, we might choose to let it dominate our thinking.

That's right, I said 'choose'.

Often, we let worry dominate us until the problem becomes enormous. The molehill really does turn into a mountain.

I used to worry about going to school, because I knew I was behind in my lessons. The problem was exacerbated because I was missing so much, and that made me fearful, so I felt ill and had time off school and consequently missed even more.

If I'd dealt with the problem differently – by facing my difficulties at school rather than running away – then the problem wouldn't have existed. But in my mind, the fear of what would happen when I couldn't do the work made me feel hopeless. I couldn't see any way out.

Elijah clearly wasn't thinking rationally. He knew God was real. He had a backstory with God. But everything was overwhelming; he was tired, and he'd had enough. Ever been there?

It's so interesting, though, because God meets him. God doesn't tell him off for not having faith. He *feeds* him so he gets stronger (see verses 5b-8). Then, although the problems haven't gone away, he has the strength to cope. He can manage the rest of his intended journey to meet with God.

Jesus was always telling people not to be afraid. He knew that's what humans do. Maybe the difference between faith and trust is faith says 'I won't be afraid' and trust says 'because I trust in you' (see Psalm 56:3). We can have faith in abstract things. I have faith my car will start tomorrow, but I can't be sure. After all, it's getting older. I often talk to it, like I talk to my phone: 'Please work!' I think maybe God would say, 'Stop praying to it, Sheila. Ask me about it instead!'

Fear says 'I believe, but...' Worry always expects the worst. Trusting Jesus doesn't mean we won't go through tough times, but we know that he's in it with us.

When my mum went to live in a care home, after developing dementia, I asked God 'why'. He didn't give me a straight answer (he often doesn't – actually, Jesus tended to ask questions rather than answer them). But he told me he was in it with me. And he was.

Being in the wilderness with just your worry for company isn't a brilliant place to be. But if you know Jesus is there with you, it makes a difference.

'The journey's too much for you. Relax, I'm here.'

Sometimes the journey is just too much for us, and we'd rather give up than fight. But God doesn't give up on us.

He's with us. He's not condemning us.

Reflection

- Do you feel overwhelmed?
- Is the journey too much for you at the moment?
- If you heard God say 'relax, I'm here!', how might that help?

Stand by for action!

Read Psalm 56, really slowly.

Now read it again.

Are there any words or phrases that really jump out at you?

Write them in your journal and say them out loud.

Conclusion

Can you imagine putting your worries in a box, just for a moment? Imagine it has 'worries' written on the lid, and you are invited to dump your worries into it for now. What would cause you anxiety about doing this? Can you *choose* to let go?

What if God was holding the box?

Lord, I'm tired and I want to let go and trust you. I can't work up faith, but I believe that you care. You never give up on me. Maybe just knowing that, is enough for now. Amen.

3

1 Kings 19:5b-9a

All at once an angel touched him and said, 'Get up and eat.' He looked around, and there by his head was some bread baked over hot coals, and a jar of water. He ate and drank and then lay down again.

The angel of the LORD came back a second time and touched him and said, 'Get up and eat, for the journey is too much for you.' So he got up and ate and drank. Strengthened by that food, he travelled for forty days and forty nights until he reached Horeb, the mountain of God. There he went into a cave and spent the night.

Have you ever felt so exhausted you just can't be bothered to do anything?

There are days when I feel like that. There's loads of stuff I should be doing, but somehow, I'd rather sit in front of the TV with a sandwich and a packet of Twiglets watching *Star Trek*.

There are also times when I want to seek God – I really do – but I just can't be bothered. I have all the good intentions. 'OK, at eight o'clock – after my favourite programme – I'll spend time with God.' And of course, I just don't.

When I was in my thirties, I had the illness I spoke about earlier, which was eventually diagnosed as Ménière's disease, a condition affecting the inner ear: it gives you vertigo so severely that you can't stand up. All you can do is lie down, not move your head, or you'll vomit. I had to put my hands over my eyes so I didn't see the swirl in front of me. And I lost part of my hearing in my right ear.

I couldn't work. I couldn't do anything. For one ten-day period all I could do was lie still in bed.

When my physical health improved, the fear of Ménière's was still there. In fact, it was a much worse problem. I had severe agoraphobia. Couldn't work, couldn't go to church.

After years of sickness, as I felt better physically, I knew it was time to try to get a job. Years of illness, just writing children's books, basically relying on my savings, hadn't equipped me for the world of work, though. How to earn money was a problem. I had such chronic panic attacks I couldn't leave the small town where I lived, and I wasn't even sure I could stay anywhere all day without panicking.

I don't know how I managed it, but I went to a church service. The speaker asked anyone who wanted to be healed to step up to the front, and as I had tinnitus – caused by the illness – I decided to do that.

I wasn't healed. But shortly afterwards, I started to praise God – not asking for anything, just praising and worshipping! Nine days later, out of the blue, someone rang and asked if I ever edited books; something I do to this day.

After this, I spent every evening, for about eighteen months, praising God. I'd go up to my bedroom at 6.30, worship for half an hour, and then hear from God. God met with me. It was no effort, being in his presence.

But circumstances changed, and life got busier. I didn't spend so much time with God. My responsibilities became greater as my health improved, and after everything, time with God began to get squeezed out more and more. 'Later, God.' But of course, later never comes.

Hence, plonking myself in front of the telly instead of being with Jesus.

OK, sometimes it's valid. I've had a stressful time with work, and I just want to zone out. But I wonder if sometimes I should just zone out with God rather than with the star ship *Enterprise*! Do I always need to talk to him? Do I always need to do anything other than just 'be' with him?

Perhaps sometimes I should just let him 'be' with me.

Elijah was exhausted. The journey was 'too much' for him. God saw his exhaustion and his need. He wasn't in the right place. In fact, he shouldn't have been there at all – God hadn't called him there. But God helped him, strengthened him, provided for him – had compassion on him.

And the strength God gave him lasted for – how long? Forty days! I don't think a sandwich and a packet of Twiglets can match that.

We need time out with God. It restores and refreshes us. A life spent on a treadmill with no time with the One who loves us best is not a life well-lived. It leads to tiredness, disappointment, burnout, depression, disbelief.

Elijah had all the above, didn't he? But there was no condemnation from God.

Just a picnic in the wilderness.

Reflection

- How much time do you spend with God per day (evaluate without condemning yourself).
- Can you let go, just 'be' with him, and let him minister to you?
- What might his 'food' be for you?

Stand by for action!

Imagine Jesus is asking you to go for a walk with him, but you just haven't got the energy. You feel as if you have a great weight, and it's too hard to keep on going.

Look at it. What might that weight be?

Put the load down, and sit. Where are you sitting? On grass? On sand?

Someone puts a picnic hamper down.

He's sitting with you. Waiting with you.

He's smiling.

It's Jesus.

What is your response?

Conclusion

God waits with us. He doesn't shout from afar off, telling us to 'get a grip'! See how he dealt with the exhausted Elijah – who actually was in the wrong place.

No condemnation or accusation.

How does it make you feel, to know that God never changes? Read Malachi 3:6a.

Jesus, I'm so grateful that although I get it wrong, and sometimes I am less than committed, you never give up on me. You don't accuse. You don't condemn. Give me strength today to receive what I need from you, as I wait with you. And you wait with me. Amen.

4

1 Kings 19:9b-14

And the word of the LORD came to him: 'What are you doing here, Elijah?'

He replied, 'I have been very zealous for the LORD God Almighty. The Israelites have rejected your covenant, torn down your altars, and put your prophets to death with the sword. I am the only one left, and now they are trying to kill me too.'

The LORD said, 'Go out and stand on the mountain in the presence of the LORD, for the LORD is about to pass by.'

Then a great and powerful wind tore the mountains apart and shattered the rocks before the LORD, but the LORD was not in the wind. After the wind there was an earthquake, but the LORD was not in the earthquake. After the earthquake came a fire, but the LORD was not in the fire. And after the fire came a gentle whisper. When Elijah heard it, he pulled his cloak over his face and went out and stood at the mouth of the cave.

Then a voice said to him, 'What are you doing here, Elijah?'

He replied, 'I have been very zealous for the LORD God Almighty. The Israelites have rejected your covenant, torn down your altars, and put your prophets to death with the sword. I am the only one left, and now they are trying to kill me too.'

Don't you just love the 'wow!' moments of life? The moments when God does something awesome?

Interestingly, though, we don't always find a deeper walk with God results from the 'wow!' moments of life.

Look at the stories in the Gospels of Jesus' miracles. He fed the 5,000 but I wonder how many of them actually chose to follow him. In fact, they seemed more interested in miracles than in actually encountering him – see John 6:26, for example: 'Very truly I tell you,' says Jesus, 'you are looking for me, not because you saw the signs I performed but because you ate the loaves and had your fill.'

I once got completely healed of a physical problem in a worship service where I was also filled with the Holy Spirit for the first time. But some of my most intimate moments with God have been in the quiet, alone; sometimes looking at nature, experiencing a beautiful view. Occasionally, we can feel awed in an extraordinary time of silence, just admiring a starry sky, for example, knowing there is something 'bigger', something 'other' than us.

A presence in the stillness.

Elijah was moaning. God doesn't answer directly. Have you noticed that about him? He points to something else, when you've asked him about that *thing* you're concerned about. So, it goes a bit like this (at least, it does for me):

'Lord, I'm worried…'

'Have you seen that flower? You call it a weed. You pull it up. But I made it.'

'Yeah – sorry about that. Look, I'm worried about – '

'You used to notice it when you were ill. You were just glad to have your sight. You were grateful to be able to see it.'

Hmm. OK. Point taken. *You took care of me then, Lord, when I could do nothing to help myself. You care about the smallest things. Why am I worrying?*

Perhaps Elijah was expecting a direct reply. Instead, God told him he would meet with him. But not quite as Elijah expected. The presence of God was about to 'pass by'. And maybe Elijah did expect the 'wow!' – the kind of thing he'd already experienced when he'd dealt with the prophets of Baal (1 Kings 18).

But God didn't speak in the wind, or the earthquake, or the fire.

He spoke in the 'gentle whisper', or the 'still small voice' (v. 12, KJV).

Interestingly, Elijah repeats his complaint – and still doesn't get a direct answer!

I wonder if I would have repeated myself. Or would the quiet voice have changed what I was going to say? Changed my view, my perspective?

So often we give God shopping lists of wants, desires, needs – and complaints – without stopping to listen. Yet this is the awesome God. The mighty Creator of all. The King.

The King who doesn't always speak in the 'wow!'.

The King who sits by my bedside when I feel ill. Who waits with me when I am scared of waiting on my own. He's the God who enjoys my company when I walk in the countryside on a sunny morning, admiring ox-eye daisies, and dog roses growing wild in hedgerows.

The small moments of life are big moments, really. The quiet moments are when we really hear that gentle voice. Yes, the great times of good worship and awesome revelation are stunning: as are genuine healings, and deliverance from all sorts of darkness.

But walking with God, waiting with God, listening to that gentle whisper... well. That's quality time.

Reflection

- Where do you most hear the voice of God?
- Are you asking God for 'wow!' moments, when he wants to whisper to you?
- How would you term 'quality time' with God?

Stand by for action!

Go for a walk (if it's cold, wrap up warmly), or wander into your garden. Find a leaf, or a flower, or a twig, or even a blade of grass.

Photograph it, paint it, look at it closely. Write a poem about it.
Whatever works for you.

Think about the God who made it.

What might he be saying to you, in this small thing?

Conclusion

It's often in the quiet moments, the small moments of life, that we really hear from God. And it might not be as we expect. He whispers, he doesn't shout.

How can we become more attuned to that whisper today?

Lord, I think I'm too busy, or talking, to really listen at times. Please help me to attune myself to your voice so I can listen to what you're saying to me – not what I want you to say, but what you're actually saying! Amen.

5

1 Kings 19:15-21

The Lord said to him, 'Go back the way you came, and go to the Desert of Damascus. When you get there, anoint Hazael king over Aram. Also, anoint Jehu son of Nimshi king over Israel, and anoint Elisha son of Shaphat from Abel Meholah to succeed you as prophet. Jehu will put to death any who escape the sword of Hazael, and Elisha will put to death any who escape the sword of Jehu. Yet I reserve seven thousand in Israel – all whose knees have not bowed down to Baal and whose mouths have not kissed him.'

So Elijah went from there and found Elisha son of Shaphat. He was ploughing with twelve yoke of oxen, and he himself was driving the twelfth pair. Elijah went up to him and threw his cloak around him. Elisha then left his oxen and ran after Elijah. 'Let me kiss my father and mother goodbye,' he said, 'and then I will come with you.'

'Go back,' Elijah replied. 'What have I done to you?'

So Elisha left him and went back. He took his yoke of oxen and slaughtered them. He burned the ploughing equipment to cook the meat and gave it to the people, and they ate. Then he set out to follow Elijah and became his servant.

I was sitting in a bluebell wood with my dog.

I was perched on a log, clearly positioned for weary travellers, because the view was wonderful. It was right over the beautiful north Essex Colne valley, lots of rolling fields, sheep, trees.

It struck me that although I had lived in the area for so long, I had never actually seen the view from that angle.

My health had improved, but I was still suffering from problems around travelling. I didn't know what I was going to do about a job. I'd spent years working in graphic design, but there was no way, back then, I could drive out of town to get a job like that.

It wasn't long afterwards that the opportunity arose, totally unexpectedly, for me to become a freelance editor, working from home.

A new view.

In effect, a new commission.

One that I could never have dreamed of.

God clearly wasn't put off by Elijah's whingeing. He had a plan for the sad prophet.

He gave him a new commission – and a new side-kick. Elisha would learn from Elijah and eventually take over his ministry; he'd have someone to walk with, talk with, share the things of God with. He wasn't asking for those things: he was just telling God how fed up he was. God saw, and provided a perfect solution.

It's interesting too how Elisha immediately 'burned his bridges', in total commitment to his new call. There was no messing around here! I wonder if he'd been praying for a new opportunity, something new, a way to serve God? Perhaps he felt a stirring inside, desiring something more than he had.

There's no condemnation here; God knows what he's going to do, and decisively does it. 'Elijah, here's the brief. OK?' 'OK!' 'Oh, and by the way, I do have people out there who still love me.' 'Ah – right.'

He tells the prophet to 'go back the way he came'.

God hadn't called him to the wilderness, and yet he had graciously met him there. He used the prophet's situation to reveal himself more fully, and to give, at this point, Elijah and Elisha a new start.

We can go off track, but we'll find God is there with us. Like a heavenly SatNav: 'Make a U-turn. I've got good things for you back there. Listen to me. Go, do what I ask. It'll be OK.'

Reflection

- Do you need a 'new view' of a situation or circumstance in your life?
- Are you feeling stirred up, as if God is calling you to something new?
- Have you ever had a time when you knew you were off track and needed to do a U-turn?

Stand by for action!

Schedule some time with God – block out an hour or so. Just to go for a walk with him, or to sit with him in the quiet. Write down your 'shopping list' of wants, gripes and needs.

Now, ask God for a new perspective on the things that concern you.

Go back to the list. Can you edit them? Edit them again.

Is there anything new that God might be saying to you? Write it in your journal.

Conclusion

Sometimes we can get off track, get stuck in the wilderness, but it doesn't stop God from working out his purposes in our lives – if we come to him. Elijah was at the end of himself, but he didn't stay in that place. God helped him, and restored his strength. God met with him, then recommissioned him.

It's a process, isn't it?

Lord, help me to just rest in you today, to hear from you, and to expect new things. As it says in Jeremiah 29:11-12, you have good plans for my life. I don't need to stress about that, or strive. Thanks that you provide all that I need. Amen.

Weekend exercise

Elijah was on a journey, as we all are. He took a wrong turn; he ran away, but it didn't stop God from meeting with him.

When we want to run from life, from circumstances, it won't stop God meeting with us, either.

Elijah talked with God about his issues, encountered him, and received a fresh commission.

It might be helpful to look up a 'labyrinth' online. This is an ancient symbol and can be useful for Christian meditation.

A labyrinth is like a maze, but it has no dead ends. The path is long and winding, but it always leads to the centre. No tricks, no cul-de-sacs. You can't go wrong with a labyrinth. Start at the opening point, and imagine yourself walking along the twists and turns. You could look at this as twists and turns in your life.

An alternative is to draw one yourself, if you are feeling creative! You could make it really personal. Illustrate it with symbols from the Gospels – a stable, loaves, fishes, a cross – you could add to this, on your 'journey', with pictures of whatever has seemed important at that stage in your life. As you reach the centre, stay still with God. Review your journey together, before turning back, and walking out of the labyrinth. What might God be saying to you about fresh perspectives?

If this idea doesn't appeal, try drawing a timeline of your life. The bits where God didn't seem to be present. Where he showed up. When you felt confident in your faith. When you doubted. You could use different coloured pencils to show how you felt at the time, or illustrate it in other ways.

How are you feeling now? Talk to God about it.

Finish this exercise by reading Psalm 121. It's a faith-affirming, uplifting psalm. Or you could write your own, based on what you have learned and thought this week.

Week 2: All at Sea

1

Matthew 14:22-31

Immediately Jesus made the disciples get into the boat and go on ahead of him to the other side, while he dismissed the crowd. After he had dismissed them, he went up on a mountainside by himself to pray. Later that night, he was there alone, and the boat was already a considerable distance from land, buffeted by the waves because the wind was against it.

Shortly before dawn Jesus went out to them, walking on the lake. When the disciples saw him walking on the lake, they were terrified. 'It's a ghost,' they said, and cried out in fear.

But Jesus immediately said to them: 'Take courage! It is I. Don't be afraid.'

'Lord, if it's you,' Peter replied, 'tell me to come to you on the water.'

'Come,' he said.

Then Peter got down out of the boat, walked on the water and came towards Jesus. But when he saw the wind, he was afraid and, beginning to sink, cried out, 'Lord, save me!'

Immediately Jesus reached out his hand and caught him. 'You of little faith,' he said, 'why did you doubt?'

There was a time when I wasn't too happy with how life was turning out. I wasn't 'done' with something that had happened to me, and wanted to continually revisit the issue. However, at that point I felt Jesus wanted me to 'move on' with him.

I can be terribly stubborn. If he was asking me to make a move, I was saying 'no, I don't want to'. What did I expect? Disapproval? In my mind's eye, I saw a hand coming over my petulant shoulder holding a chocolate bar. I had to laugh. I knew it meant Jesus would wait with me till I was ready to move.

Moving on in whatever way – physical, emotional – can be scary. It can be like getting out of a boat and walking on water, our eyes fixed only on the One in front of us.

Peter is such a character. He gets it wrong, but he also gets it right. Here, he seems to be the only disciple willing to take a chance, to take a risk, and to do something impossible. Jesus invites him. He says, 'Come on, Pete!' And Peter obeys: 'Right, if Jesus says come, it'll be fine!'

It is… until he takes his eyes off his Lord.

But he knows what to do. He calls on Jesus, and he's rescued. I wonder if Jesus said what he did with a smile.

At least Peter *tried*. I can't believe he wasn't scared, but he took a risk. He took a step. He rather neatly, and not without getting wet, found out that he could do amazing things, if his eyes were on Jesus. But when he shifted his focus and looked at the unpromising circumstances instead, he got in trouble.

I've had many times in my life when I've let the circumstances overwhelm me, just like the waves threatened to overwhelm Peter. These are real waves, not just imaginary ones. Real troubles. Debilitating illness. Agoraphobia. No work. A parent with dementia.

OK, I've had a few waves that aren't terribly serious. The hoover packing up. Not able to find the spanners for my mower. A flat tyre on my car. Irritations.

When I had agoraphobia I just didn't go to places where I felt I wouldn't be able to manage. Oddly, I felt quite safe in the middle of a field with just my dog for company. Eventually life became so small I went for walks with my dog, and that was about it. I wouldn't take a step outside of my comfort zone, but that zone was tiny.

You don't risk drowning if you don't leap into the water. But living with fear as your master leads to a small life.

Not that living a small life is always as bad as it may seem. A small life gives you a different perspective. When my sight had been affected by Ménière's, it was wonderful to just be able to see again the tiniest, most insignificant flower. Yes, the day of small things should not be despised (Zechariah 4:10). Indeed, sometimes God leads us there.

But there may come a time when he says 'time to move on'. Moving on, getting out of the boat, seemed frightening to me. But he beckoned me on; so I took the step.

Is God asking you to do that too, and waiting with you till you say yes? 'My Presence will go with you, and I will give you rest', says the Lord (Exodus 33:14). Perhaps you'll reply with Moses: 'If your Presence does not go with us, do not send us up from here' (v. 15). In other words, 'I'll move if you say so, I'll even take a step out of the boat, but I'm not going if you're not there!'

'Don't worry. Trust me!' he says. 'Why do you doubt my love for you?'

Whether you've got that sinking feeling through circumstances, or you're just too scared to take a risk, remember: all you've got to do is lift your head just a little to see Jesus; to see his hand coming down to help. Maybe it won't hold chocolate. Perhaps he's just waiting to pull you back up onto safe ground, back into the boat; or perhaps he's asking you to walk on water with him to wherever he wants to lead you. And that's the point. It's where he *leads*.

Reflection

- How would you describe your life today? A gentle stream, a stagnant pond, a raging storm?

- How do you usually react when it's a raging storm?
- Is Jesus asking you to 'walk on the water'? In what way?

Stand by for action!

Find a seascape – in a magazine or on the internet – that seems to describe your current position. If you're artistic, draw or paint it. Put a boat in the picture. Where is it? In the storm? Becalmed? Happily sailing along? Stuck? Shipwrecked?

Imagine Jesus walking on water, alongside.

Where are you in the picture?

What does Jesus say to you?

Conclusion

Acknowledging that we often sink under the pressures of life, albeit momentarily, is honest and real. We want to walk on the water, looking at Jesus. But we often just don't want to take that risk.

Jesus, if you want me to get out of the boat, then help me to hear your call and obey, trusting you to take care of the situation. Lord, I don't want to look down at the waves, I want to keep my head up, looking at you. Amen.

2

Luke 22:31-34

'Simon, Simon, Satan has asked to sift all of you as wheat. But I have prayed for you, Simon, that your faith may not fail. And when you have turned back, strengthen your brothers.'

But he replied, 'Lord, I am ready to go with you to prison and to death.'

Jesus answered, 'I tell you, Peter, before the cock crows today, you will deny three times that you know me.'

If you know the rest of the story, you may be smiling to yourself, 'You'll never let Jesus down – yeah, right!'

Peter is going to deny Jesus. But at this point he doesn't think he will. He's quite good at bravado. He hears from God (Matthew 16:15-17) but also lets his own voice get in the way (v. 23).

We each hear from our own selves, God and the enemy; we may also still 'hear' the voices of others who may have spoken to us in negative ways long ago, and that label has stuck.

Peter clearly believed that Jesus would triumph. He was the Messiah, after all, who would rid the nation of the occupying Romans. But he wasn't the sort of Messiah Peter and others were expecting. He'd set people free, for sure. He'd rid the people who came to him of everything that stopped them being in relationship with a holy God. But he had to die first. It was his death that would buy the people freedom: the sacrifice in our place that would mean humanity no longer had to be separated from their Creator.

Peter had a robust faith in Jesus, but a lot of his own desires, thoughts and feelings were overlaying his beliefs.

I think we often do this with God, especially when we first start our journey with him. It's almost as if we think of him through a filter of our own imaginings. It's only when we start to know him, to walk with him and talk with him and listen to him that he begins to reveal who he really is, reshaping our thoughts, our minds.

'OK, Jesus, you never promised I'd have an easy life. I get that. When I first became a Christian I thought perhaps you'd bless me with that perfect partner, big house, great job. Didn't quite factor in that you'd want me to live in this area… be single… have to give my job up…'

Are you disappointed? Is the Christian life not quite as you thought it would be? Are there promises you believed God made to you, but they haven't happened yet? How do you cope with that?

When I was feeling disillusioned over a particular area of my life, God pointed out that things aren't always as they seem. I see things from my own perspective, but he sees the bigger picture. The true picture. We need to trust him.

Jesus knew what Peter would do. But look at what he says in Luke 22:32: Peter would turn back and encourage others. Jesus had a bigger view of Peter's life than Peter did. It was a different perspective.

Let's believe Jesus' version of our lives, his view, not our own, our past, other people's viewpoints or opinions, or the enemy's negatives. These things can shrivel our view of ourselves, causing us to fear moving 'out of the box' in case we make a mistake, get it wrong. We all lash it up. When we fall down, let's get up, say sorry, receive his forgiveness, and keep walking.

Fear of failure can stop us seeking relationship with God. But he knows us. He knows we're going to trip up. And he still loves us!

I think Jesus is looking for the good in us: the good fruit (John 15:16).

Reflection

- Do you give too much room to voices that aren't God's – including your own?
- In what way does turbulence in your own life muddle up what God might be saying to you?
- What does it mean to you that Jesus has a bigger view of your life than you do?

Stand by for action!

Review the day, or, if you're reading this early on, think about the day before. Ask Jesus to show you something he is pleased with. Write what he says in your journal. If you don't feel he says anything, come back to it later, and see if he has spoken to you as you re-review.

Who do you know who speaks encouraging, uplifting yet honest words into your life? Can you arrange to spend time with them?

Conclusion

God really does have good plans for us (Jeremiah 29:11-12). But verse 13 says this: 'You will seek me and find me when you seek me with all your heart.' So, what's the key to hearing from God today?

Lord, I want to hear from you. I want to know your ideas, your thoughts. Help me to see how much you love me, and to love others as I am loved. Amen.

3

Luke 22:54-62

Then seizing him, they led him away and took him into the house of the high priest. Peter followed at a distance. And when some there had kindled a fire in the middle of the courtyard and had sat down together, Peter sat down with them. A servant-girl saw him seated there in the firelight. She looked closely at him and said, 'This man was with him.'

But he denied it. 'Woman, I don't know him,' he said.

A little later someone else saw him and said, 'You also are one of them.'

'Man, I am not!' Peter replied.

About an hour later another asserted, 'Certainly this fellow was with him, for he is a Galilean.'

Peter replied, 'Man, I don't know what you're talking about!' Just as he was speaking, the cock crowed. The Lord turned and looked straight at Peter. Then Peter remembered the word the Lord had spoken to him: 'Before the cock crows today, you will disown me three times.' And he went outside and wept bitterly.

Peter has really messed it up. He's denied Jesus. Jesus knows it.

It can be really hard being a Christian – especially in a non-Christian environment.

I had been out of work for months when I first came to Christ. After a while, I got a new job with a graphic design firm, and was earning well. I liked the people I was working with.

But after a few weeks, the boss asked us to work on a magazine that was all about the occult.

I didn't know much about following Jesus back then, but I did know that this was something I couldn't work on. It was lies, untruth, it would lead people astray. I knew that because I'd been heavily involved in some of the practices; especially astrology.

Then a wise Christian told me that when we honour God, he honours us (1 Samuel 2:30). So I told my boss that I simply could not work on that material. I expected him to fire me.

Instead, he listened and said he didn't want to compromise my faith. To cut a long story short, I didn't have to work on that magazine. I stayed with the company for six years. It was a good time.

So, I learned early on that God really does honour his people when they take a stand for him. But it isn't always easy. There are times I have said things I wish I hadn't, and times I haven't said things and then wished I had.

Sometimes, it's better to keep quiet and listen – to people, yes, but also to God's 'still small voice' (1 Kings 19:12, KJV).

I once started to chat to someone I didn't know. I thought, 'What a great opportunity to share about Jesus!' but felt the Lord tell me not to say anything about him. It turned out the person in question would have found it very difficult to hear anything about 'God' just then. Yet I felt a strong impression to tell them that they were in the right place at the right time. They seemed very comforted by that. They didn't know it was God who was encouraging them, showing his love to someone who was dear to him but not near to him.

It certainly made me think.

He loves people.

We let him down. We turn away. Sometimes we don't want to know him at all. But he never gives up on us.

He didn't give up on Peter and he won't give up on you.

'Don't be afraid,' he says. 'Don't hide from me, like Adam and Eve did right at the start. Bring it to me. Everything. I love you.'

Reflection

- How do you feel when you know you've let God down?
- Do you ever feel afraid to come to him? Why? Why not?
- Can you bring 'whatever it is' to him, let it go, leave it with him?

Stand by for action!

Read Revelation 3:20.

Lay a table. Put down two plates, two mugs or glasses, knives, forks, spoons; you might like to dress the table with a vase of flowers.

Imagine you and Jesus are going to have supper. Or it might be you and Father, or the Holy Spirit. You could lay the table for four!

As you wait for your guest/s to arrive, how do you feel?

What might the conversation be like?

There's a knock at the door...

Conclusion

Does it surprise you that Jesus wants to spend time with you?

Do you want to spend time with him?

Psalm 46:10 says: 'Be still, and know that I am God'. We hear his voice, don't we, in the stillness. But maybe that isn't *always* necessarily a physical stillness. Perhaps it's an ongoing attitude of the heart.

Rushing through life, we can soon begin to feel disorientated. And then we can make mistakes, start panicking, and even turn away from the One who calls us to be with him.

We need to slow down. Breathe. Take time to admire a clear blue sky, or listen to raindrops falling. This is the moment we're alive. Right now.

Jesus, you are good, and you love me. I bring to you [whatever troubles you]. Thank you that you understand. Help me to hear your voice today, and honour you in everything I say and do. Amen.

4

John 21:1-6

Afterwards Jesus appeared again to his disciples, by the Sea of Galilee. It happened this way: Simon Peter, Thomas (also known as Didymus), Nathanael from Cana in Galilee, the sons of Zebedee, and two other disciples were together. 'I'm going out to fish,' Simon Peter told them, and they said, 'We'll go with you.' So they went out and got into the boat, but that night they caught nothing.

Early in the morning, Jesus stood on the shore, but the disciples did not realise that it was Jesus.

He called out to them, 'Friends, haven't you any fish?'

'No,' they answered.

He said, 'Throw your net on the right side of the boat and you will find some.' When they did, they were unable to haul the net in because of the large number of fish.

When nothing makes sense, everything is a mess, what do we do?

Peter has seen his best friend – the friend he had denied knowing, three times – horrifically murdered. The Easter Saturday experience of loss, shock, had devastated him, compounded by the fact that he knew he had let Jesus down so badly. Then there was the empty tomb. And Jesus... alive...

Not exactly ordinary times. Can you imagine the myriad of emotions being felt by Peter and the rest? What turbulence! Nothing Peter had experienced when fishing in the worst storms could have prepared him for that.

Life is unfathomable!

So what does he do?

Like many of us, he goes back to the comfort of the familiar.

There are times when we seem to be doing well. Everything is running smoothly. There are interludes when the sun seems to shine especially for us as we relax on the patio of life. It's when there's a rumble of thunder in the distance and then lightning strikes that we scurry back indoors.

Peter's life has been turned upside down. Fear, denial, death, intense grief, then amazement. What a rollercoaster ride!

What's your go-to comfort, when there's turbulence in your life? Mine used to be horse riding but these days, a safer option is watching TV. It's a switch-off, an: 'I can't deal with it right now, so I'm checking out for a while.' Can't pray, too tired, too confused. Put the telly on.

Your 'go-to' bolthole might be similar. Or it could be work – like it obviously was with Peter – or something generally good like a sport, gardening, walking, or even dancing, or theatre, or going out for a meal. It could be returning to some kind of addiction you actually hate and at times think you've conquered, but it's always lurking, waiting to reel you in as soon as you have a weak moment.

It's interesting to think about where we go to, in our minds, when life gets tough. It might be the past. It might be an imagined future. Or we might join in with someone else's story, as I tend to do when blobbing out in front of my preferred science fiction.

We go where we feel comfortable. Accepted. Safe. Even when at times it isn't particularly 'real'.

Peter had given up fishing. Jesus had made him a fisher of people (Matthew 4:19). Out of the old life, into the new!

And back to the old, when things didn't make sense.

Back to what it was before Jesus made this ordinary fisherman something special.

But in all the turmoil, Jesus was there. Right in the middle of it.

An unsuccessful night's fishing results in a shout from the shore. It's Jesus, repeating a miracle from early in his ministry. In Luke 5:1-11 he had instructed the disciples just where to catch fish when they simply hadn't been able to... On this occasion, their nets had begun to break, but interestingly, after Jesus' resurrection, and his call to put the nets down again, they *didn't* break. The catch was huge, but nothing seems to have been broken.

It's like Jesus was not only identifying himself here, but reminding Peter of his call on his life: 'You really are a fisher of people, Peter; it's not over! I'm not revoking your call. Yes, you're broken. But I'm making you whole. And you'll have a real catch, Peter. Watch and see.'

Reflection

- What makes you run to that place that you lived in before Jesus called you? Disappointment? Grief? Fear? Something else?
- Romans 11:29 says that God's calling and gifts are 'irrevocable'. Think about that.
- This time, there are no broken nets. God is in the business of making us whole. Where do you need his restoration?

Stand by for action!

Choose a new page in your journal, and write down all the negative things that you feel at times when life is overwhelming. Leave a space in the centre of the page. If you are particularly artistic, you might prefer to draw or construct a painting or collage.

In the middle of the words or picture, write the word 'Jesus'.

Can you turn your eyes from the 'stuff' of life, the One who is the Life?

Conclusion

Fear doesn't like being faced. But even if we're in the maelstrom of anxiety, we're not alone. When we feel all at sea, it's good to know there's someone in the boat with us (see Luke 8:22-24).

Lord, when I feel as if I'm drowning in a sea of anxiety, please help me to stand, to take a few deep breaths, and to look up and realise you are here. Amen.

5

John 21:15-17

When they had finished eating, Jesus said to Simon Peter, 'Simon son of John, do you love me more than these?'

'Yes, Lord,' he said, 'you know that I love you.'

Jesus said, 'Feed my lambs.'

Again Jesus said, 'Simon son of John, do you love me?'

He answered, 'Yes, Lord, you know that I love you.'

Jesus said, 'Take care of my sheep.'

The third time he said to him, 'Simon son of John, do you love me?'

Peter was hurt because Jesus asked him the third time, 'Do you love me?' He said, 'Lord, you know all things; you know that I love you.'

Jesus said, 'Feed my sheep.'

So, Jesus is alive, and he's made breakfast on the beach for his friends – the very same ones who ran away and left him when he was arrested, even though some of them promised they wouldn't do that: namely, Peter.

He cooks the breakfast and then he invites Peter to go for a little walk.

I wonder if Peter expected a rebuke. Perhaps he was thinking, 'Uh-oh. Here it comes.'

But all Jesus does is ask him a few gentle questions. The same one, actually, three times – remember, Peter denied Jesus three times.

The Greek uses different words for love. The Greek word Jesus uses here on the first two occasions is referring to the highest form of love, God's love, unconditional, all-encompassing, undeserved *agape*. Peter replies twice that he loves Jesus like a brother. Not the same word. But then, he could hardly tell Jesus that he loved him with everything he had, could he? He knew he didn't! That had been proven.

Interestingly, on the third mention, Jesus comes down to Peter's level. He asks him if he loves him like a brother.

Jesus comes down to our level with such compassion. He became a man, he walked with us, talked with us, showing us what God would be like if he had a human face.

And he gives Peter a new commission; or perhaps, an extension of the old. He's going to take care of the Good Shepherd's flock. And I don't think that meant that Jesus expected him to switch from fishing to farming.

Jesus as the Good Shepherd is a beautiful picture – read John 10:1-18. There are echoes here of Psalm 23, the famous psalm of the boy who would be a king, but who also knew what it was to be a shepherd. The psalm talks about fearing no evil (v. 4). I don't suppose sheep do. They wander about, eating grass. The shepherd takes care of them. Sometimes the sheep wander off, and may get bogged down in all sorts of soggy ground. But the shepherd rescues them – making a point of going after the one who is lost (Luke 15:4-6).

The sheep know their shepherd's voice (John 10:4). It's a great metaphor for our lives, when we know Jesus.

If we listen out for the voice of Jesus and become familiar with it, then we'll be more attuned to his presence. Any 'voice' that doesn't match up with what Jesus says in his Word, of course, needs to be ignored. God won't tell us to do something that is clearly not what he teaches in his revealed Word to us.

But there are times when we don't know what to do, and the answer doesn't seem to be too clear from the Bible.

A few years back, I had a cancer scare. Friends were kind. Someone said that medical science was great these days, and if I did have something scary, it would surely be OK. Others talked about God's healing, and naming it and claiming it. But I just wanted to hear from Jesus.

I went for a long walk in the meadows near my house and watched the butterflies flitting around the harvested fields. I sat on a straw bale and looked at the dark August trees.

Then he spoke.

'Nothing that happens will alter my plans for you.'

That's all it took. I was in his hands. And I felt peace.

As it turned out, thankfully I was fine.

Sometimes we just need to hear that quiet voice, the one that reassures and comforts, the one that doesn't shout at us for our mistakes, or tell us we're failures, or weak, or useless.

God's voice is the voice of love.

Reflection

- How do you think Peter felt when Jesus restored him, and gave him a new commission?
- When you come to God, do you expect a loving embrace, or a harsh word?
- What commission has God given to you, that doesn't seem to have been fulfilled yet? Talk to him about that.

Stand by for action!

Go for a walk, if you can. Ask God to speak to you, but don't intentionally set out to 'hear from him'. Just enjoy the walk, wherever you go. Stop and look at blossom, buttercups, autumn leaves, winter skies – according to the season! When you come home, note in your journal anything that struck you as interesting, or different somehow. How might God be speaking to you in that?

If you are unable to go for a walk, read through Psalm 23 and take an imaginary stroll in quiet meadows. Again, carefully observe what you see. Then write it down, and ask God what he is saying to you.

Conclusion

Practising recognising God's voice takes time. But as we do take that time, he will speak, and we will find ourselves hearing from the One who loves us more and more. There may be times when he is silent. Maybe he is waiting for us to say sorry for something, or put something right, if we can. Or perhaps he just wants us to be still and quiet and just 'be'. It can be helpful when we remember there's not always a need to talk.

Lord, thank you that you love me so much. I'm sorry when I get it wrong. But I know you restore and renew. Help me to learn to listen to your voice today. Amen.

Weekend exercise

When we feel as if we're alone, that we've done too much for God to ever forgive, or we just don't understand what's going on, in the turbulence and stress and 'stuff' of life, he's still there.

If we can just begin to listen to him, to be in that attitude of stillness, even when life around us may seem to be anything but calm, we can start to live our lives from the position of rest in him and all that he is.

Think of a stair lift. It goes up and down, carrying someone who might struggle with stairs. It takes the weight of that person. It moves, even though the person is resting. How can we begin to see our lives in Jesus as riding on that stair lift rather than charging up and down stairs and feeling exhausted?

Is there a chair in your home which you can place in a quiet spot, a chair where you can be alone with the Lord? Somewhere you can go with the intention of meeting with him? If you can be outside, is there a particular bench in a park or garden?

As you sit down, imagine yourself placing your weight on Jesus, resting in him. Note in your journal any thoughts that come, but don't worry if none appear. Just be comfortable with your divine Companion in the silence. Silences can be silences of companionship. Good friends don't always have to talk to enjoy each other's company. In fact, silences can be a sign of a deeper relationship, where chatting doesn't have to fill in any awkward gaps in conversation.

Week 3: Not Seeing Clearly

1

John 20:11-15

Now Mary stood outside the tomb crying. As she wept, she bent over to look into the tomb and saw two angels in white, seated where Jesus' body had been, one at the head and the other at the foot.

They asked her, 'Woman, why are you crying?'

'They have taken my Lord away,' she said, 'and I don't know where they have put him.' At this, she turned round and saw Jesus standing there, but she did not realise that it was Jesus.

He asked her, 'Woman, why are you crying? Who is it you are looking for?'

Thinking he was the gardener, she said, 'Sir, if you have carried him away, tell me where you have put him, and I will get him.'

Mary has seen her friend, her Lord, crucified. And now it seems that someone has stolen his body, so carefully laid in the new tomb of the wealthy Joseph.

The characters around the cross and afterwards are very interesting: John, Jesus' mother, other women – but it's Mary, here seen hovering about in the garden (once the disciples had seen that the tomb was indeed empty and had gone away, puzzled!) who is the one who sees the risen Jesus first.

Perhaps it's because she waited. She waited at the empty place. The place of sadness and sorrow. The grave. The grave that actually should have had a body in it, but the body was gone.

Mary's hopes were buried and now stolen, too. The One who had come to set people free (John 8:36) had freed this woman (Luke 8:2), given her a fresh start, but now all her hopes were in the dust.

She sees angels. I wonder if she fully realised what she was seeing, in her distress. If I was faced with a couple of angels I wonder if I would have had a normal conversation of any sort! But Mary's grief has blinded her.

Life can become so intense at times that we don't really know what we're doing. Anxiety does that, too. If it begins to spiral out of control, it blocks out any reasonable thought.

Have you ever looked into clear water, at the reflections? Beautiful, calming, peaceful. But when you're looking into a flowing woodland stream, it's not quite the same. We think we see something in the water, but is it just a reflection of a tree? Is that green patch in the water up ahead a reflection, or a water lily? The picture isn't clear. The turbulence can seem to muddle things up.

Mary is about to encounter Jesus, but she doesn't recognise him. True, she wasn't expecting to see him... alive, at any rate. Or he may have disguised his appearance. It seems his body was very different, after the resurrection. And yet it bore some similarities (see John 20:24-27).

Jesus doesn't introduce himself. He says, 'Why are you crying?' – the emphasis being on her. He asks her a question: who is it she is looking for?

Who are we looking for?

Are we looking for a dead Jesus?

Or a Jesus happily in a manger in a stable, a baby, which we can smile about once a year, while opening our presents?

Or are we looking for a close encounter with a real, living person, who is God?

That's life-changing, isn't it?

Reflection

- Think about your view of Jesus. Is he a baby? Is he a man? Is he a far-away religious figure? Is he dead? Is he alive?
- Who are you looking for – really?
- If you're finding life stressful right now, what would it be like to hear Jesus asking you why you are crying, sad or worried?

Stand by for action!

Whatever time of year it is, think of the spring.

I love blossom trees. I planted an ornamental cherry tree near my sundial on the lawn. It's beautiful in April. I planted it there so I could always see beauty, even if I was ill and unable to move out of my own living room. I wanted to see something fresh and lovely, even if I was in a difficult situation.

Write in your journal the things you like about springtime. Paint or draw, if you are artistic. Write a poem, if you are creative, or a song. What does springtime represent in general, and for you personally?

Conclusion

In the middle of a garden where there was only brokenness and endings, waiting in the emptiness, new hope appears. Sometimes God does that. Something has ended, and something new is beginning. At times we have to let go of old expectancies, old ways of being, to embrace something new.

It might be an unexpected or even unwelcome change. We have to grieve the past, for sure, but we can't live in a tomb – empty or not.

New life appears in the garden, just as springtime brings flowers to the earth and buds to the trees.

Lord, thank you for fresh starts. Help me to not to look for the living among the dead (see Luke 24:5). You are alive, and I am alive. This is the moment for life. Help me to enjoy this moment and to feel your love. Thank you, Jesus. Amen.

2

John 20:16

Jesus said to her, 'Mary.'

She turned towards him and cried out in Aramaic, 'Rabboni!' (which means 'Teacher').

I remember a particular visit with my mother, who lived in a care home for more than thirteen years until her death. I hadn't seen her for a while, for one reason or another – including problems caused by the Coronavirus pandemic. I sat there, with a mask on, and gloves, and an apron, and Mum sat opposite, in her wheelchair, quite cheerful, cuddling a teddy bear.

I couldn't help but think about her as she was before she got ill; she wouldn't even go to the shops without wearing her earrings! Dementia, Parkinson's disease, and other health issues had all taken their toll.

After an hour of chatting to my mother, who was in a sunny mood, I realised that she actually didn't know who I was. I told her I was her daughter. She expressed surprise that she had one. Then she said she thought I was just a nice lady who had come to talk to her.

Although I always knew this day would come, when it happened, it hit me hard.

My mother didn't know who I was.

But of course, I knew who she was.

And even when we don't recognise God in our situation, whatever that might be, he knows us. By name.

Isaiah 43:1 says: 'Do not fear, for I have redeemed you; I have summoned you by name; you are mine.' Redeemed – bought back; something that has been lost has been reclaimed. Summoned – called by our own name. And told that we are his own: we are accepted, we belong.

How wonderful to understand that we are known by name – individually. When we pray, we aren't just sending prayers 'up there' hoping they'll come into land with some remote God who has to look up our address before he can reply.

When Mary heard Jesus speak her name, she must have been astounded. Apart from the fact that here was a man she had seen die a brutal death, he was actually standing there, calling her by her own name.

Do you ever wonder if God is really hearing you? Frantic prayers don't always seem to be answered. Or perhaps they are, in a way we haven't seen yet, or in a way we are not expecting.

Sometimes I pray, but then I tell God what I want the answer to be! Yes, there's a place for being specific, but it takes faith to leave the outcome with Jesus, without telling him exactly what to do and how to do it, in fine detail.

Waiting on God can mean just that: *waiting*. I don't always do 'waiting' very well. Waiting is a strange place to be: like waiting for a phone call, checking that you haven't missed it, wondering if there's something wrong with the phone, the line, the service provider...

Doubts begin to mount.

When we start to doubt his presence, his goodness, his love, the spiral downwards can lead to real anxiety.

In that garden, unexpectedly, the distraught and confused Mary met with the Master who called her by name.

In the middle of her distress, he was there, and personal.

We need to remember that he always is, even if we don't encounter him in quite the way we expect, or get the answers precisely in the way we're asking for.

Reflection

- Redeemed. Summoned. Accepted. Belonging. Which of these words means the most to you, right now?
- How well do you do 'waiting' when you feel your prayers are going unanswered?
- If we really, *really* believe that Jesus cares personally, how might that allay anxiety?

Stand by for action!

Spend some time with Isaiah 43:1. Imagine God the Father, or Jesus the Son, or the Holy Spirit – whichever you feel comfortable with – saying this to you. He breathes your name. If we truly believe we are his, how might that affect our prayer life? Journal any thoughts.

Conclusion

To hear our name spoken, especially by someone we love, is very special. It makes us known; it brings with it a sense of belonging, or being accepted. When God speaks, we may expect him to add a rebuke after our name, especially if we were used to that sort of thing when we were children. But when God speaks our name, it's in love.

Lord Jesus, when you spoke Mary's name her world had been turned upside down. Speak my name today, and put my heart at rest. Amen.

3

Luke 24:13-24

Now that same day two of them were going to a village called
Emmaus, about seven miles from Jerusalem. They were talking
with each other about everything that had happened. As they
talked and discussed these things with each other, Jesus himself
came up and walked along with them; but they were kept from
recognising him.

He asked them, 'What are you discussing together as you walk
along?'

They stood still, their faces downcast. One of them, named
Cleopas, asked him, 'Are you the only one visiting Jerusalem who
does not know the things that have happened there in these days?'

'What things?' he asked.

'About Jesus of Nazareth,' they replied. 'He was a prophet,
powerful in word and deed before God and all the people. The
chief priests and our rulers handed him over to be sentenced to
death, and they crucified him; but we had hoped that he was the
one who was going to redeem Israel. And what is more, it is the
third day since all this took place. In addition, some of our women
amazed us. They went to the tomb early this morning but didn't
find his body. They came and told us that they had seen a vision
of angels, who said he was alive. Then some of our companions
went to the tomb and found it just as the women had said, but
they did not see Jesus.'

This is one of my favourite stories in the Bible. I simply love the fact that
Jesus joins in with these people on their walk, but they're not 'seeing'

him. He asks a few pointed questions, drawing them out, but doesn't actually say, 'Hey, it's me!'

Have you noticed how God doesn't just say 'Hey, it's me!' but reveals himself quietly, and sometimes very slowly?

Jesus turned up on earth and didn't immediately announce that he was God in the flesh (John 1:1; Colossians 2:9; Hebrews 1:3). He showed who he was by 'signs', as John is keen to point out in his Gospel (John 2:11).

When I look back on my life, I can see periods where God has drawn very close to me and I have said, 'I don't want to be any further away from you than I am right now.'

But I can also remember arid times where God's presence didn't seem to be anywhere near. Seasons of doubt, and believing only because I was hanging on to Jesus' own promises of who he was; days when I've had to sit with not understanding, of not 'getting' why God doesn't *do* something. Or at least, doesn't do what *I* want him to do in that situation.

I was sitting on a bench in a village churchyard. I'd visited the recent grave of someone I had known well. I'd just heard of someone else who had passed away, too, and it was beginning to feel unbearable.

Where was God, in all this loss and distress?

'Jesus, please, where are you?'

It was a summer's afternoon, peaceful and still. I'd been for a walk with a friend; there were blood-red poppies scattered in the cornfields; swaying barley, looking like waves, hissing in the gentle breeze. Beauty in the midst of such sadness.

Now resting by the warm church wall, looking at the fields ready for harvest, and vast Essex skies, people came by and spoke – people I knew but didn't expect to see there that day. It was uplifting. A sprinkling of light in the middle of a dark time.

I felt as if God had planned the afternoon, right to the very bench my friend and I had chosen; it was only later that I realised it was the very bench my granny had sat on years before and had her photo taken, on a particularly happy occasion.

Life is a mystery. It can be confusing, disorientating, lonely, and at times, overwhelming. I felt it that afternoon.

But while I didn't have any big answers that day, I came home with a quiet sense of knowing that God had been present all along. He hadn't vacated his heavenly seat. I just hadn't recognised his presence.

I had to admit that he must have a bigger plan than I could see or understand.

The two disciples on the road to Emmaus had clearly had their world turned upside down. The man they had expected to 'redeem' their country had died; and then there were stories of a missing body, angels, and the Saviour being alive. Can you imagine how confused they were?

And now, here's this stranger, coming alongside, asking questions. It's quite amusing to hear the almost irritated comment in verse 18: 'Where have you been, my friend, that you don't have a clue what's happened here?'

Even in the strangest moments, the grief, the distress, we can often miss the sound of another, a Friend walking with us.

The sound of his steps may get louder as we walk. We may not have recognised him at first, but he's there.

Perhaps he's asking you to sit with him. To just 'be' for a little while; breaking up the journey with a time of rest.

Reflection

- Who walks with you that you don't always acknowledge?
- What questions do you think Jesus might ask, if he was taking a walk with you, or sitting on a bench in a quiet place?
- What would you reply?

Stand by for action!

If you drew a timeline in Week 1, review it now. Is there a specific place (or places) where God really met with you, and things were never the same again?

If you haven't drawn the timeline, think back. What was the most life-changing encounter you've had with God?

Write a poem, a song, draw, or just thank God that he is there for you now, and he has never left you.

Conclusion

So often we don't 'see' Jesus, yet he is right here with us. He hasn't abandoned us. He never will!

Lord, I'm sorry for the times when I think you're not there and you really are. I'm sorry for my doubt. You love me. You walk with me. Help me to lean hard on you, Jesus. Amen.

4

Luke 24:25-27

He said to them, 'How foolish you are, and how slow to believe all that the prophets have spoken! Did not the Messiah have to suffer these things and then enter his glory?' And beginning with Moses and all the Prophets, he explained to them what was said in all the Scriptures concerning himself.

I used to take part in quite a lot of street evangelism, and that brought some very interesting encounters, especially at night-time, in a large town.

I, and the other people in the team, would get into some seriously deep conversations about the nature of who God is.

We want people to see Jesus, don't we? To see him clearly. So, we need to trust God to reveal who he really is to people who are looking for spiritual reality. I think gently pointing to Jesus and his own words – particularly, for me, in the Gospel of John – is very helpful. Jesus said he was the only way to God: 'I am the way and the truth and the life. No one comes to the Father except through me' (John 14:6).

Evangelism is about invitation; inviting someone to look at the claims of Jesus for themselves. This may involve discussing them, examining them, but ultimately people need to make up their own minds about what to do with any revelation they receive.

An invitation. An invitation to meet with the One who said he was the truth, and the life.

I once had a dream about a beautiful garden, which was alive with small creatures, insects; there was a river with fish in it, the sky was teeming with birds, and there was a tree with fruit. Jesus was in the middle of this garden. Anywhere he is, there is life.

Inviting someone to meet with him is inviting them to meet with life.

Philip did this, when he went to tell his friend Nathanael that he and his other friends had found the One he believed had been prophesied about. John 1:43-51 makes good reading. Nathanael is so authentic in his cynicism. You can almost hear him, under that tree, saying, 'Oh yeah? I'll believe it when I see it.' Much like Thomas in John 20:25: 'Unless I see the nail marks in his hands and put my finger where the nails were, and put my hand into his side, I will not believe.'

Yet both of these 'doubters' exploded into faith when Jesus revealed himself to them.

Honest seeking, honest doubts. God is big enough to handle that. And he is big enough to reveal himself to those who look for him. When we call out to him, he will tell us things we didn't know (Jeremiah 33:3).

Nathanael believed when Jesus revealed he had insight into what Nathanael had been doing, even though Jesus hadn't been there in person; a supernatural revelation. Thomas believed when he saw the evidence of who Jesus really was: the dead man, living again. And he declared, 'My Lord and my God!' (John 20:28).

It's all in the Scriptures, who Jesus is, and what he came to do. His Spirit breathes life into the word, so it becomes living. The Word of God is 'alive and active' (Hebrews 4:12). How can it not be, when it's the Word of the 'Living One' (Revelation 1:18)?

Sometimes we think we have to provide all the answers when people who are looking for the reality of God ask big – and sometimes awkward – questions. But in truth, we just have to invite them to meet the same person we have already come to know.

'I know this man Jesus. Take a look at what he said about himself. Talk to him. He'll reveal himself to you. Let me know what happens.'

That's facilitating a space for God to work in their lives.

Reflection

- How do you share your faith?
- How do you respond to Jesus' claim of being the only way to God?
- John 10:10 says: 'I have come that they may have life, and have it to the full.' Jesus is speaking here. What do you think he meant?

Stand by for action!

What are the images that come to mind when you think of 'life'?

How do these images reflect what you know of Jesus?

If Jesus is *life*, what would it be like to spend an afternoon in his company? Boring? Would he do 'religious' things? Would he be laughing? What do you think?

Make a note of any thoughts.

Conclusion

Jesus was interesting to be around. If he hadn't been, he would not have attracted the company of so many. The Gospels clearly show us what he was like, as a man. Inviting people to consider who Jesus really was, what he said and what he came to do is inviting them to join in a conversation. A conversation that can lead to a life-changing encounter.

Lord, when I think life is all about me, help me to remember that it isn't. It's all about you. It's not about my fine words or clever arguments. It's about your invitation to know you and walk with you. Thank you, Lord. Amen.

5

Luke 24:28-35

As they approached the village to which they were going, Jesus continued on as if he were going further. But they urged him strongly, 'Stay with us, for it is nearly evening; the day is almost over.' So he went in to stay with them.

When he was at the table with them, he took bread, gave thanks, broke it and began to give it to them. Then their eyes were opened and they recognised him, and he disappeared from their sight. They asked each other, 'Were not our hearts burning within us while he talked with us on the road and opened the Scriptures to us?'

They got up and returned at once to Jerusalem. There they found the Eleven and those with them, assembled together and saying, 'It is true! The Lord has risen and has appeared to Simon.' Then the two told what had happened on the way, and how Jesus was recognised by them when he broke the bread.

I love eating with friends – or people who may soon become friends.

When we sit down and eat with someone, it's a relaxing, friendly thing to do. It's the laughter, the discussion, it's the sense of ease around a good meal that makes it an enjoyable time.

If I'm worried or nervous, I find my appetite disappears. What about you? I was thinking, one day, about what it would be like to have dinner with Jesus. Food is a real theme in his Word. Just read the Gospels, and Revelation – see for example 3:20, which we looked at earlier in this book.

Jesus doesn't invite us into fear. He invites us into faith, and companionship.

I once imagined having a meal with Jesus, and was surprised to find myself sitting in a pretty grotty café. It seemed then that Jesus was asking me if I was happy with this, or if I wanted something better.

Next minute I felt we were in a classy restaurant. Plush carpets, white linen tablecloth – a table for two, laden with good things. And as he leaned across the table, offering me the basket of bread, the sleeve of his white robe rolled back, and I saw the nail print in his wrist.

Maybe that's what happened to the disciples as they were about to eat with him. They hadn't recognised him – in truth, they had hardly been expecting him. But he seems to have hidden his identity from them until this point.

He takes the bread and gives thanks and breaks it and gives it to them, reminiscent of the Last Supper. Maybe that's what they remembered. Or perhaps they recalled the feeding of crowd, where he thanked God for the loaves and fishes that were miraculously able to feed so many people (see for example Matthew 6:41).

I would love to have seen the expression on their faces, wouldn't you? Then he disappears.

Sometimes I feel his presence, but then I don't. I suspect we will only feel his continued presence when we are face-to-face with him in Glory. It takes faith to believe he's here with us when we can't see or feel him close by. In those times, when we *do* choose to believe, then I think that pleases him.

When we know he's with us, our anxieties can't stay in the room. It's a bit like being in the dark and switching on a flashlight, or lighting a candle, and watching the shadows flee away. Nothing of the darkness can stand in the presence of the One who is himself the light (John 8:12).

Whatever gnaws at us, whatever whispers its negativity, whatever brings doubt, simply cannot be in the same place as Jesus Christ, the Son of God.

I have a picture on my living room wall, of a town, with the lights on; it's evening or maybe early morning. But as you look at the brighter horizon, you see that the picture, all dark blues, is actually not as dark as you might think on first glance.

Life seems like that at times, doesn't it? Dark and scary. But with Jesus, maybe we can begin to believe that there are possibilities of light.

Yes, there are still questions – just as there were for the disciples on the road to Emmaus; more questions than there are answers, at times.

But for those people, life, which had just got very much more complicated, had now become much, much bigger in all its possibilities: because Jesus was alive.

Surely, that can also be true of us.

Reflection

- Jesus invites you into companionship. How do you respond to that?
- What anxieties are in the room of your life right now?
- How does the recognition of Jesus being alive alter the possibilities in your life?

Stand by for action!

Jesus said: 'I am the light of the world. Whoever follows me will never walk in darkness, but will have the light of life' (John 8:12).

Imagine walking along a dark road. But you look up. There's the moon, and stars, and you remember who put them there (Genesis 1:16).

Perhaps things aren't quite as dark as you thought.

Someone is walking alongside you. You can see his face in the moonlight. In fact, as you look at him, you realise it is more twilight than dark; maybe it's even morning.

The One who walks with you is smiling at you. You realise the light is coming from him, himself.

What happens next?

Conclusion

If we know God's presence, his light and life, comfort and companionship, even in the middle of dark times, can lead us and guide us. Just because we don't always see clearly, it doesn't mean that Jesus isn't there. And although our view of him can be muddled and muddied, it doesn't stop him being who he is – ever-present and walking with us through our lives. Sometimes all we can hold on to is Jesus. Even when he seems to disappear!

Lord, thank you that you love me. I don't always understand, and I don't always see you in the situation, but I believe you're there and you love me. Amen.

Weekend exercise

Over the weekend, try to read through Psalm 91.

I first came across this psalm when I was just fourteen, with virtually no church background. I was scared – I couldn't see a way out of my immediate predicament of being in a school where I felt I was out of my depth. Then God spoke to me in this psalm. He told me that I needn't be afraid. He was there.

At that time, I didn't know what it meant to know God. I didn't understand that he was inviting me to walk with him. It took many years for me to see more clearly that I could be his friend, and that he already was mine; that I needed to rest in who he was and what he had done for me.

Go through the psalm slowly. The first line, for example, has a proviso – if you want to 'rest' in God, then you need to 'dwell' in him – much as Jesus asserted in John 15:5: 'I am the vine; you are the branches. If you remain in me and I in you, you will bear much fruit; apart from me you can do nothing.'

Think about what this means for you. What does it mean to 'dwell' in God's shelter? How can you do that more and more?

It might be that other verses appeal to you – when you find one that 'jumps out at you', stay with it. Mull it over. Don't let it go. Ask God what he is saying to you in this.

Journal your thoughts.

Week 4: Freedom Comes

1

Acts 16:22-24

The crowd joined in the attack against Paul and Silas, and the magistrates ordered them to be stripped and beaten with rods. After they had been severely flogged, they were thrown into prison, and the jailer was commanded to guard them carefully ... he put them in the inner cell and fastened their feet in the stocks.

One day I went to see my mum in the care home, having just come back from a weekend away. It was a lovely break, and I told her all about it. These were in the days before the sliding down into another level of dementia meant she forgot who I was.

I felt so sorry for her, lying there in her bed, unable to walk or even bear her own weight. There'd be no more holidays for Mum.

Then I asked her if she remembered Jesus.

'Oh yes,' she said, and her face lit up. 'He never leaves me. When I feel his presence, it gives me such joy.'

After the visit, I sat in the car for a few moments; it humbled me, knowing she was richer than many people, even though you would never think it.

She knew his joy.

Paul and Silas are telling people about Jesus in Acts 16. But Paul believes there's some kind of spiritual problem with a slave girl who is following them about. She's actually declaring the truth about them (see Acts 16:17) but discernment is needed. She might be saying the right thing, but it isn't coming from the right source; the fact is, not all so-called spiritual 'wisdom' is from God.

The slave girl's owners, furious that they can no longer exploit her (she was fortune-telling, and making her owners a lot of money doing so – see Acts 16:16), drag Paul and Silas to the authorities.

Consequently, they are stripped, beaten, flogged, thrown into the inner cell of the jail, with their feet in stocks.

They are well and truly bound.

The girl, of course, was also bound; bound to some dark dominion that was controlling her, as well as under the control of her owners. Paul, in Jesus' name, told the darkness to go, and it did. She was free of that influence. I wonder what became of her.

And now, because of this, Paul himself is in trouble.

Sometimes, we can feel as bound as Paul and Silas. We may find ourselves feeling as if our feet are in stocks; we may even know, as they did, that it is our own words, actions, decisions, or life choices that have put us there.

As we will see, this wasn't the end of the story for Paul and Silas; and it isn't the end for us.

My mother was bound. And yet she was also free, somewhere on the inside. Physical freedom would one day follow the spiritual freedom she already had – the same freedom you and I have, if we know Jesus. Because however bound we may feel or actually be, Jesus is the One who has the keys to our freedom (John 8:32).

My mother died in the autumn of 2021. The last time I saw her, she was lucid – and incredibly, she knew me. We prayed together and I sang a hymn: she joined in with the chorus. Her health and strength had left her, but the Lord never did. He gave her joy, even within the bounds of illness.

'Paradox' is a word that seems to perfectly fit living in an imperfect and often frightening and distressing world, yet also knowing the joy and confidence that being a citizen of the kingdom of God brings.

Reflection

- Have you been in darkness, and someone has come alongside and helped you, in Jesus' name, to experience freedom? Thank God for them now.
- What does it mean for you to know that your story hasn't ended?
- What is your hope for the future?

Stand by for action!

Get some wool, or string, and wrap it tightly around a piece of card, or wood, or a tennis ball. As you wrap it, think of the things that seem to keep you bound: fear, anxiety, anger – whatever else. Talk to God about it. This might be a brief chat, or lengthy 'unloading'. Don't rush to finish. Say all you want to say. Then, unwind the wool or string. This might be something you want to do immediately; it might be tomorrow or another time. Do it when you feel ready for 'release'.

Conclusion

Let's thank Jesus that he sets people free and declares his favour (Luke 4:18) – that is, his free, unmerited, unearned grace (Ephesians 2:8-9). We might feel that we are bound up, or in a prison either of our own making or of someone else's. Whatever our situation, let's take a moment to look into the eyes of Jesus, in whom there is freedom, hope and joy.

Jesus, I would like to know your freedom and joy today! I want to be free, Lord, on the inside. I want to walk into the destiny that you have for me. I know you'll never leave me. Thank you, Jesus. Amen.

2

Acts 16:25-34

About midnight Paul and Silas were praying and singing hymns to God, and the other prisoners were listening to them. Suddenly there was such a violent earthquake that the foundations of the prison were shaken. At once all the prison doors flew open, and everyone's chains came loose. The jailer woke up, and when he saw the prison doors open, he drew his sword and was about to kill himself because he thought the prisoners had escaped. But Paul shouted, 'Don't harm yourself! We are all here!' The jailer ... brought them out and asked, 'Sirs, what must I do to be saved?'

They replied, 'Believe in the Lord Jesus, and you will be saved – you and your household.' ... the jailer took them and washed their wounds ... The jailer brought them into his house and set a meal before them; he was filled with joy ...

Stuck in a prison cell, in stocks, you would have thought that Paul and his companion would be terrified, feeling abandoned and alone.

Where was God, in this situation?

They'd been working for him, hadn't they?

And now this had happened.

You wouldn't blame them for being angry with God, would you? Annoyed? Disillusioned?

'Well, Paul, wasn't expecting this.'

'Me neither. We'll never get out.'

'Why didn't God protect us?'

'Dunno. I'm terrified. Have you seen the size of those rats?'

No, this isn't how they react. They pray. And they sing God's praises! Someone once challenged me to think about my internal dialogue.

What's my self-talk like? I quickly realised it was pretty negative. I tended to have arguments with people who weren't even there.

'Hmm. She upset me. Next time I see her, I'll say this. And she'll say that. And I'll – ' By the time I finished working out who would say what, I'd be pacing the kitchen, really worked up! These imaginary conversations never seemed to be very life-enhancing.

Better to focus on Jesus, and praise him, even when I would actually *rather* be fuming over something and plotting what I'd say in a situation that would probably never happen!

Sometimes, praise just releases us. Maybe it's when we put God in his rightful place in our lives, the top place, the first place, and begin to really acknowledge who he is, that he breaks in on our behalf and 'does stuff'. That's not the reason to praise him, of course. We should praise him because of who he is, not because of what he does for us, or to get something from him.

And sometimes, of course, we can praise him in the midst of trouble, and the trouble remains, even though we may feel more of a sense of his peace and presence in it.

On this occasion, though, he worked fast to release Paul and Silas, and a whole household came to know God. Interestingly, Paul's concern is for the well-being of the jailer, then the jailer returns the favour. And there's that word again: 'joy'.

Some of the trickiest circumstances we may experience may actually be for the benefit of someone else. There may be a bigger, far-reaching purpose in what we're going through. Hard to see at the time, it can be one of those things that are only seen from a distance – as we look back over our lives. Or, sometimes, we may never understand 'why' this side of heaven.

God doesn't always deliver us in the way we would have hoped, and we have to acknowledge that. Even if he doesn't – can we still trust him (Daniel 3:17-18)?

Reflection

- How's your thought-life? Generally positive? Or negative?
- How can you remind yourself to turn your thoughts to Jesus?
- Can you trust God that a difficult situation might be for someone else's long-term benefit?

Stand by for action!

What keeps us locked up, locked in, and what releases us? What sets us free?

Where do we feel fear, and where do we feel peace?

What's your internal dialogue like? Is it helping, in releasing you from fear?

Choose a new page in your journal, and write your typical inner dialogue on the left-hand side.

Bring what you have written to God, and ask him to help you replace old, destructive thoughts with new, good ones.

On the right-hand side of the page, write down scriptures or words of affirmation that come to mind as an alternative to the negative thoughts. Ask God to help you choose the positives from his Word when the old dialogues try to reassert themselves.

We read in 2 Corinthians 10:5 that we should 'take captive every thought to make it obedient to Christ'. It might help to imagine taking negative thoughts captive in a net, or a jar, or in a box, putting them aside, and physically turning from them, choosing to 'think different'. For example: 'I can't do this' could be replaced with: 'Thank you, Jesus that "I can do all [things] through him who gives me strength"' (Philippians 4:13). It will take time, and is a discipline, but if we are aware of the negativity and keep reminding ourselves to stop giving so much room to old thoughts, it will help us maintain our peace – even in difficult circumstances.

Conclusion

Choosing to praise, thank and focus on God when we want to run about in circles freaking out is a hard thing to do. But remembering Paul and Silas, their attitude, and what God did in their situation, is very heartening. If they *hadn't* praised, would they have been set free – and would the jailer and his family come to know God?

Lord, I choose to praise you in my circumstances today! Forgive me when I choose not to look up, but look down or at someone else, or even myself. Thank you that you are God, and you are worthy of my praise. Amen.

3

Acts 8:9-24

Now for some time a man named Simon had practised sorcery in the city and amazed all the people of Samaria. He boasted that he was someone great ... But when they believed Philip as he proclaimed the good news of the kingdom of God and the name of Jesus Christ ... Simon himself believed and was baptised. ... When Simon saw that the Spirit was given at the laying on of the apostles' hands, he offered them money ... Peter answered: 'May your money perish with you, because you thought you could buy the gift of God with money! You have no part or share in this ministry, because your heart is not right before God. Repent ... and pray to the Lord in the hope that he may forgive you ... For I see that you are full of bitterness and captive to sin.' Then Simon answered, 'Pray to the Lord for me so that nothing you have said may happen to me.'

It seems strange, doesn't it, to want fame for fame's sake? Maybe it's not always about money and lifestyle. Perhaps sometimes people desire fame because they want to be noticed, be special.

Trying to 'be' someone can be an exhausting exercise. It can also be quite fake. I once bought a young pear tree but it was only when I found an apple growing on it that I realised it had been in the wrong wrapping!

Sometimes we try to be something we're not, don't we? But it's hard to keep up the pretence – to live up to what's on the wrapping, when it isn't really 'us'.

Trying to 'be someone for God' can also be exhausting.

When I was first ill, I was disappointed that I couldn't achieve my dream of working for God. Sitting by the fire – even moving my head might give me a dizzy spell, and that frightened me – I told God that 'all I wanted to do was work for you'. He spoke quite clearly: 'I don't want you to work for me. I want to do my work in and through you.'

At that time of enforced rest, I couldn't do anything much except take my dog for walks when I felt physically OK, but I grew in the understanding that God has many people who want to do wonderful things for him, but maybe not so many who just want to sit with him – be his friend.

Simon, in the story, clearly needed to 'be someone'. He needed to be admired as a great man. When he saw what the disciples were doing through the Holy Spirit, he actually offered them money for the gift.

Why?

Nothing to do with relationship with God; we can't buy God's gifts any more than we can buy his love – or anyone else's. No; it appears he wanted people to admire *him*. He wanted the gifts so that he could impress people.

His attitude revealed that he had little real understanding about what it really meant to know Jesus; what it meant to be a follower, in relationship with God.

In a sense, he was as locked in a prison as Paul and Silas were, in Acts 16; a prison that he probably didn't recognise.

Sometimes we don't recognise the 'prison' that we're in, either; a prison of performance, perhaps, where we try to impress, dress, look the right way, in order to be thought of as special. If we get it wrong, if we're ignored – does that mean we don't count? That we aren't important?

Are you scared of rejection?

You're special to God – *chosen* (John 15:16). Chosen to bear fruit; fruit comes from staying in the Vine (John 15:1-4). We can't bear the fruit of the Spirit on our own (Galatians 5:22-23). It's *fruit*. It comes from 'abiding' in Christ (KJV).

Abide! Rest.

You matter! Not what you wear, what you look like, what great achievements are on your CV. You, yourself!

Reflection

- What do you think of Peter's response to Simon?
- Simon asks Peter to pray for him (v. 24). What does that indicate to you?
- Do you feel special and chosen by God?

Stand by for action!

What does it mean to you that God wants your friendship?

Write a letter to God, as you would to a friend. It can be as long or as short as you like. Tell him what you want to tell him, ask what you want to ask.

How do you think God might reply, if he wrote back?

Conclusion

People's harsh or negative evaluations of us – who we are, our looks, or our capabilities – or lacking the affirmation we feel we need, can lead to a loss of self-worth and fear of rejection. We may feel as if we don't 'measure up'. Isn't it freeing to find we don't have to 'measure up' to the God who calls and chooses us?

Lord, thank you that I don't have to stress to be 'good enough' or 'special'. I am special to you. Thank you that I am free to be myself in you. Amen.

4

Luke 23:34a

Jesus said, 'Father, forgive them, for they do not know what they are doing.'

God often speaks to me by showing me 'pictures'. He sometimes talks to me through images of water, which is ironic, as I really don't 'do' boats, or swimming.

On one occasion, I felt I was on a bridge, looking at the flow of water beneath me. It was a lovely stream, trickling sweetly along. I could see some deep parts, where fish swam in the depths, near the riverbank, but the rest of the water was shallow, tinkling over stones and rocks.

Hang on – there were quite a few rocks.

It was a picture of my life! And the message was clear. The stream might well be happily burbling along, but it wasn't actually flowing as it should. Did I really want to live in the shallows?

I could see the riverbed clearly now, and some of the rocks were quite big.

One was very big indeed. And dark.

It occurred to me that the rock could be swept away if the river was a raging torrent.

But wait – did I really want that? Wasn't I happy having that rock there? Was I tolerating it, or even *holding on* to it?

Living in the shallows is like living a half-life of compromise. I didn't want to live like that. So I knew I needed to let the rock go.

What does that rock represent for you? It may be different from 'my' rock.

It could be idolatry – someone or something is more important than God, for you. Or it could be something else... such as unforgiveness.

Unforgiveness is like a heavy, dark rock in the middle of our hearts. It can poison everything – attitudes, conversations.

We need to forgive.

Sometimes people don't know what they're doing, or have done, to us. They simply don't understand the full effect. And sometimes they do. Our natural response can be anger, a need for that person to understand just what they've done: essentially, to make them feel our hurt. But we have to accept that people make choices, those choices can hurt us, but that we also have a choice – whether to let resentment poison our lives, or to let go of it; to move forward with Jesus, or to keep carrying that boulder of bitterness.

Jesus forgave the very people who were killing him.

If we look at the Gospels, Jesus talks a lot about forgiveness; it's really key to walking closely with God.

Some of the teaching is quite sobering. For example, Matthew 6:14-15; Matthew 18:21-35. But as we read the story of the lost son in Luke 15:11-32, we get a glimpse of the nature of God, and the forgiveness he is so ready to bestow. If we are forgiven by such love, surely we can let that forgiveness flow to others? We will find, by letting go of bitterness, we can know a new freedom in God. It's not easy, though; and forgiveness doesn't always mean full restoration with a person or relationship that has been damaging, or damaged.

Still, if we want the freedom God has promised us, we need to get rid of any 'rocks' that potentially inhibit our relationship with him.

Unforgiveness can keep us from living in the flow of life that God wants us to have. I know that unforgiveness kept me bound for a long time. It was only when I forgave that I began to feel real release from life-limiting fear.

In truth, we may not want to let go of some of those rocks of unforgiveness. They may feel comfortable. We can be used to them. But if we really want to be free, it means letting go.

Letting go started me on the road to freedom. But I'm aware that there are rocks of all sorts still on my riverbed, and I also find they accumulate! It's something I need to keep a constant eye on. It's so easy to let a small rock of hurt feelings escalate into something that really damages my heart, my life, and my walk with Jesus and others.

I believe God wants us to step out of the shallows, and allow that raging torrent of his Spirit to flood our lives, washing away anything that is a barrier to our freedom, so that we can walk in his presence without fear.

If we imagine ourselves caught up in such a flow, we might initially feel frightened of where it may take us. As a strong flow of water can change the course of a river, so the flow of the Spirit unleashed in our lives could potentially change our own course. But how exciting! Who knows where the powerful, peaceful and loving current might take us?

Don't let anything rob you of that life and freedom. Especially not a dark rock.

Reflection

- Are you living in the shallows?
- What's the dark rock in your life?
- Is there someone you need to forgive? Do you need to forgive yourself?

Stand by for action!

Can you ask the Holy Spirit to come and flood your life?

Isaiah 46:4-5 says: 'There is a river whose streams make glad the city of God, the holy place where the Most High dwells. God is within her, she will not fall; God will help her at break of day.'

Make it personal.

'I am the holy place where he lives.'
'He is within me.'
'I will not fall.'
'He will help me.'

Maybe one of these statements means more to you than the rest. Write it out, on Post-it notes or pieces of card, and place it where you will see it often.

However, you may find that there is something stopping you from either asking or experiencing the flow of the Spirit. What is it? Can you bring it to God? If you don't know, ask the Spirit to show you. If you find it too difficult to 'let go' of any particular hurt, perhaps share these issues with a trusted friend or Christian leader or spiritual director. Sometimes we need help on the journey!

Conclusion

When we ask God to forgive us, and then forgive others, we might feel that 'dark rock' of unforgiveness is still there. We need to ask the Spirit to come and wash that thing away. We may find it takes some time to feel truly forgiven, forgiving or free. Don't worry. At times feelings need to catch up with spiritual reality. And truthfully, forgiveness can be an ongoing and lengthy process.

Father God, please take away any dark rocks of unforgiveness that stop the flow of your Spirit in my life. Help me to forgive to be free. Thank you. Amen.

5

John 4:7-10

When a Samaritan woman came to draw water, Jesus said to her, 'Will you give me a drink?' ... Jesus answered her, 'If you knew the gift of God and who it is that asks you for a drink, you would have asked him and he would have given you living water.'

My grandparents had a big garden. In those days, people seemed to have fairly structured ideas around gardens; a lawn, flowerbeds, vegetables, some currant bushes, and perhaps an apple or pear tree.

Beyond that was usually a shed. And behind the shed... a compost heap. The part of the garden they didn't want anyone to see.

I can remember having tea with my family on the neat lawn. We never took tea round the back of the shed, balanced on the rubbish heap.

It struck me one day that we often invite Jesus to tea on the freshly mown (possibly nicely striped) lawn, with the best china and fancy cakes, but we rarely invite him round the back of the shed.

I'm pretty sure he wants to see that grotty, unkempt part. The part we try to hide. The part we're afraid to show him. Will he reject us if he knows about...?

It's like the idea of my life as a house.

'Come into the living room, Lord. I've just – '

He looks at a cupboard door.

'No, not that door, Lord. I'd rather you didn't...'

He's still looking at the cupboard, but he won't force it open.

Yet, there could be something toxic in there that is affecting the whole house.

He wants us to invite him into those areas of our lives that we try to pretend aren't there.

Jesus is very good at getting to the point.

We can see this with the woman at the well. He opens the conversation with a request for help. What an icebreaker.

He then tells her he knows her story (vv. 16-18), something she clearly isn't proud of. She evades answering; she's out at midday drawing water alone because she's trying to avoid gossip and, perhaps, unhelpful remarks about a life that she seems ashamed of.

Jesus knows about 'the bit behind the shed' or the secret cupboard, but he doesn't condemn.

He lets her know that he knows – but she's accepted. And because he accepts her, it means a new acceptance from her community (vv. 28-30,39-42).

Jesus doesn't exclude. He invites.

If we really believed that, we wouldn't be afraid to come to him with the tricky bits of our lives.

Adam and Eve hid from God when they messed up (Genesis 3) and we tend to do the same. We might try to cover ourselves with inadequate bits of foliage – 'It wasn't my fault, Jesus. It was that person/that situation/ the way I was brought up' – but let's be honest with God.

He knows our faults and failings.

He forgives. He restores.

And he still loves us!

Reflection

- What do you imagine the woman might have been thinking when Jesus revealed that he knew her story?
- Do you have an untidy place behind your 'shed', or a 'cupboard' that Jesus is asking you to let him sort out?
- Can you let him into that place?

Stand by for action!

Find a drawer or cupboard or something else that needs tidying up. It might just be rearranging a shelf in the kitchen. As you do so, ask God to speak to you. You might be very surprised by what he will say as you remove old tins, or remember good things that you had forgotten.

Afterwards, think: What did you chuck out, and why? Was it old 'stuff' from the past you didn't need to keep? Did you find anything useful or interesting that you had forgotten about?

Are there areas of your life where you know Jesus wants you to experience more of the freedom he offers?

Is there something good about yourself that you might need to be reminded of?

Conclusion

'The fear of the LORD is the beginning of wisdom' (Proverbs 9:10, KJV). That's a healthy kind of awe, and it's right to have that level of respect for God. But let's not be frightened to let him into our lives, our hearts, those very places where we know we need help.

Father God, you invite me into friendship with you. You know my secrets, and you aren't condemning me. Help me to let you into those places where I need your special help. Amen.

Weekend exercise

In my living room, I have a large expanse of glass. I also have a mirror on the opposite wall.

So if I look in the mirror, I can see directly behind, right into the garden.

It's incredible how different the garden looks from that viewpoint. It looks beautiful – like someone else's place! Normally, I just see weeds, nettles, all the stuff that needs sorting out, mowing, hacking down.

Another perspective can be very helpful for seeing things in a new way. A new angle can show us something we are used to seeing, but in a new light.

Sometimes it's good to look at ourselves in a different light. Old thoughts can keep us locked up, locked in. We need to break out of that, see ourselves as God views us, and have the confidence to invite him to do what he wants to do in and through us, so we can walk in the freedom he wants to bring.

Fear and anxiety must leave when we realise just how important and special we are to God. Meditate, if you can, on this verse: 'I have chosen you and have not rejected you' (Isaiah 41:9).

Journal any thoughts.

Week 5: This is the Day

1

Matthew 6:25-27

Therefore I tell you, do not worry about your life, what you will eat or drink; or about your body, what you will wear. Is not life more than food, and the body more than clothes? Look at the birds of the air; they do not sow or reap or store away in barns, and yet your heavenly Father feeds them. Are you not much more valuable than they? Can any one of you by worrying add a single hour to your life?

I was living life at 100mph. I realised I was just too stressed when one morning, while watching the Sunday service being livestreamed from my church, I was also dealing with washing, housework, and consequently racing up and down the stairs.

I needed to get away, if only for a day.

To be honest, I didn't feel like going on retreat. It felt too hard to seek God. What an effort! It was all I could do to just turn up. I didn't even have the energy to pray. I wasn't sleeping well. Have you ever had times like that, when your mind is in such a whirl you just can't rest?

I decided I'd sit in the room I was allocated for the day and watch the birds on the feeder just outside the window. Then, as I watched, thoughts dropped into my mind.

The birds weren't worried! God had made them. He knew what they needed. He'd created them. They were his responsibility.

Could God be speaking to me, when I was too tired to do anything other than simply turn up?

I went for a walk round the expansive grounds. Coming to a bridge, I looked down at the quiet waters. I felt it was important to be 'in the now' of life; enjoying the moment. How often I don't do that, and how refreshing it is when I remember its importance! For, after all, the 'now' is where God is – the 'I AM' (Exodus 3:14), the ever-present eternal.

At that point I was reflecting on Psalm 139:1: 'You have searched me … and you know me.'

You know, Lord.

He knows all about me. All my troubles. My joys. The good and the bad. He knows all my thoughts (Psalm 139:2). Everything. I belong to him. It's a two-way relationship when I often think of it as one-way: me doing all the asking, the stressing, the worrying… I forget that I'm in relationship with Someone bigger than me, Someone who actually *made* me. I'm his. Although he gives me free will, and I can choose to run from him, when I commit my life to Jesus, then I'm his responsibility.

It's good, in particularly stressful times, to try to regain our focus. To stand back and take a deep breath and give ourselves the opportunity to see clearly.

When I was unable to travel due to agoraphobia, I made a 'happy board'. I stuck lots of pictures of things I liked – traction engines, thatched cottages etc. – onto a board and would look at them when I felt low. But I didn't concentrate on just one picture. If I had, I would have missed everything else. It would have been as if that one was the only picture on the board.

We can focus so much on one thing that is troubling us that we miss the bigger picture of what's going on. It's another question of perspective. Worry focuses the vision solely on the problem. Everything else fades away. The worry or fear then seems to become enormous, and sometimes way of proportion.

Anything we concentrate on to the exclusion of all else takes on a distorted position within our life. We need to get our eyes off the worry and remember that we're in a two-way relationship with the One who made us – who knows us, and who really cares about us.

Sometimes we can be too exhausted by the 'stuff' of life to do anything other than simply turn up and be available for God to speak.

But maybe, just maybe, that's all that's needed.

Reflection

- Can you remember what you were worrying about a year ago? If you can, what happened, and was the situation resolved? If you can't – does this tell you something about the nature of worry?
- Are you focusing on one problem in particular so that it's crowding out everything else?
- Do you feel you can just 'turn up' for God at times – with no agenda?

Stand by for action!

Write out Jesus' words in Matthew 6:25-27 on a big piece of paper, or on a fresh page of your journal. Underneath, make a list of the things that are worrying you the most, with the biggest worry at the top. When you've finished, look at the list. God's words are above it. God is above it. Remind yourself that he is greater, and that you can trust him.

Pray through the worries, not telling God how to deal with them, or your desired outcome. Thank God that he has heard you.

Then go and do something you enjoy, even if it's just looking at a favourite picture or photo, admiring a view, taking a walk.

If this seems like too much bother, skip everything and just make a cup of your favourite beverage, savour the taste, and sit quietly.

Just turn up. Be available.

And see what happens.

Conclusion

God knows us. He cares. He knows *you* and what worries you. He comes alongside, and says, 'Let's walk through this together.' We need to let go, and lean on him. Sometimes, in the middle of our troubles, that's all we have the energy to do. But he's there, he's real, and he's committed to us.

Father, thank you that you care about my smallest worries, and my biggest concerns. Whether it's a little problem or a big one, you are bigger than them all. Help me to trust you with my whole life. Amen.

2

Matthew 6:28-32

… See how the flowers of the field grow. They do not labour or spin. Yet I tell you that not even Solomon in all his splendour was dressed like one of these. If that is how God clothes the grass of the field, which is here today and tomorrow is thrown into the fire, will he not much more clothe you – you of little faith? So do not worry, saying, 'What shall we eat?' or 'What shall we drink?' or 'What shall we wear?' For the pagans run after all these things …

When the pandemic hit in 2020, I remember going into my local supermarket and watching people piling their shopping trolleys with loo rolls, baked beans and pasta. I saw the fear on their faces as they crammed as much as possible into their bags – this was before restrictions came in about how much we could buy!

I have to admit, I bought way more pasta than usual (!) and am currently still working my way through it.

During the pandemic, I noticed my own fear. I sat back and had a good think about it.

What was I actually afraid of? Could I name it? Was it a particular thing, event, or situation? Or was it like 'the void' I mentioned earlier – an empty space of some sort, an *unknown*? Was I scared that God would abandon me?

Where was my faith?

True, I was unnerved by the circumstances. But I was also in fear of what hadn't actually happened yet; and what God may never allow.

I remembered when I was ill. God looked after me then, and the sense of security I knew in him as I watched him come through for me at that time had deepened my faith.

Perhaps your fears or worries are around provision. I know what it's like to be out of work with no prospect of a job, not knowing how I'd ever be able to make a living. I also know what it's like to live with someone who has undiagnosed dementia, and to be frightened of what the next day would bring.

Life is uncertain, and unless our hope is anchored in something that can never be shaken (Matthew 7:24-27) we'll be tossed about like a small ship in a storm when things 'go wrong'.

Life is also about choices. We can start to panic, or we can turn to God, remember his faithfulness, and tell him that we choose to believe he will not let us down.

The more time we spend with a friend, the better we know them and the more we can trust them. The more time we spend with God... do you see my point?

Reflection

- How much does the news, or social media, influence your mood?
- Do you tend to panic first and pray second? What do you think might happen if you chose to pray first?
- Have you ever experienced a miracle of God's provision – big or small? Can you write this down, or even tell someone about it today, to encourage you and them?

Stand by for action!

Sit quietly in your favourite place. It could be your sitting room, your bedroom, your living room, or outside, on a park bench, or in your own garden. It could be the place you chose to sit in the weekend exercise of Week 2.

Breathe deeply. What can you hear? What can you see? Touch something – a piece of wood, your dog, your cat, a cushion. How does this feel?

This is the now, the immediate moment.

Any worries about the future, imagine putting them in a bag. You can look at them later. Anything that comes to you from the past, put that in the bag too.

Quietly repeat: 'This is the day the LORD has made; [I] will rejoice and be glad in it' (Psalm 118:24, NKJV).

Stay in this attitude of peace and acknowledgement of who God is, for as long as you can.

When you stand up, raise your hands, if you can, or look up. Blue skies or grey, the sun is above them. God is with you. Seek him first.

Conclusion

Beyond my back garden is a main road. Sometimes the sound of traffic drowns out the birdsong. That's why it's good, in the summer, to throw open the window early, and listen to the dawn chorus, and the nearby crowing of a cockerel, before the busyness of the day masks the sweeter songs.

The sounds of life threaten to drown out our hearing God. But the most important thing we can do is to hear from him; to find the tangible presence of the One who is himself 'our peace' (Ephesians 2:14).

Lord, help me to find your peaceful presence today. Help me to find that first, and to stay there; to seek you first, to put you first, and to trust that you have everything that concerns me in your hands – that all will be well. Amen.

3

Matthew 6:32

... and your heavenly Father knows that you need them.

When I was about nine, we went on holiday to Cornwall. We were staying in a little chalet, one of a small group on a farm. The holiday also involved riding ponies, so I was happy; I was totally horse-mad.

One of the children I'd made friends with asked if I'd like to go fishing with them. My parents gave their permission, but I had to be back at the chalet by 8pm. We set off through the woods to a pretty spot by the stream, and my friend fished.

At about quarter to eight I began to think about going back to the chalet. I wondered if I was going to be able to find my way; I decided to just follow the path and hope for the best.

As I set off, I was suddenly aware of someone coming down the path towards me. It was my dad, hands in pockets, whistling softly; he'd come to fetch me.

I felt so protected and loved at that point. And relieved!

My earthly dad *knew* that I needed him to walk with me, otherwise I'd probably finish up getting very lost.

My heavenly Father knows my needs too – and is able to protect, provide and be there for me in a way no human being can.

Of course, not everyone has had a good experience of fatherhood, but every one of us can know the Father who adopts us as sons and daughters, when we come to him (John 1:12). If it is just too difficult for you to think of God in these terms, remember, he is also the greatest Friend we could ever have.

I've walked through woods of uncertainty, doubt and despair; sickness and fear. When we can't see a way out, when we peer into the future and wonder what on earth's to come, we can feel lost, alone and very scared. Our eyes focus on the trees; the problems, the issues that are crowding in. We can't see the path home. We lose sight of the One who accompanies us.

In Luke 10, we read the story of Martha and Mary, and Jesus' visit to their house. Mary was listening to Jesus' teaching. But Martha was so frazzled with all the work she had to do when Jesus came to visit, she finished up asking the question many of us do when we take our eyes off him: 'Don't you care ...?' (Luke 10:40).

Life's circumstances often mean we look away from him and find anxiety grabbing at us as his presence seems to slip further and further away.

'Don't you care, Lord?' comes at the tail-end of a process that leads us away from trust. And that is a place of anguish.

'Don't you care?'

'Yes, I do. Can't you see me coming towards you, to walk you through this?'

Remember, it's about relationship – and that's two-sided.

We might feel lost, but we're in relationship with Someone who has promised never to leave us (Hebrews 13:5). And he's with us right *now*, in this present moment.

Reflection

- God knows your need.
- God wants to be involved in whatever troubles you.
- God cares.

  How do you respond to each of these statements?

Stand by for action!

Imagine you are walking in a beautiful wood. Or, if you prefer, on a coastal path, or across meadows. What is the weather like? What are the sights, the sounds, the smells?

You suddenly realise that you don't know the way home.

Do you cry out to your heavenly Father?

Or do you keep going, hoping to find your own way out of the situation?

Has the weather changed? Or stayed the same?

Are there any signposts? What do they say?

Is there someone coming along the path to help you?

Journal any thoughts. Did you feel the presence of God? When was it the strongest?

Conclusion

God knows our needs – and he knows what to do to get us through the difficulties. At times he might remove the problems altogether, but at other times he walks with us through them. It can be hard to see how God could bring good out of bad situations and yet this is what his Word says he will do. Romans 8:28 tells us 'in all things God works for the good of those who love him' – if he is good, then how can he do anything less (Psalm 100:5)?

Lord, sometimes I just don't see how things can work for my good, or anyone else's, and I get anxious about that. But you know my need. You know everything I do, and what lies ahead. Help me to put my hand in your hand, as we walk together. Amen.

4

Matthew 6:33-34

But seek first his kingdom and his righteousness, and all these things will be given to you as well. Therefore do not worry about tomorrow, for tomorrow will worry about itself. Each day has enough trouble of its own.

When I was in my twenties, I greatly enjoyed riding horses cross-country. But one day, a horse ran away with me. It was terrifying. I was praying like crazy and hanging on for all I was worth.

Sometimes that's what life can feel like, isn't it?

It was OK in the end, the horse stopped and I got off, unscathed – but pretty shaken up. It was not a day I would want to repeat.

I've also had times when a sudden invitation has meant that a day that might have been ordinary and uneventful has been unexpectedly fun-filled and exciting.

Worrying about tomorrow is pointless. We have no idea if there will be a horse bolting, so to speak, or whether all will be calm, or even exciting. We aren't there yet so we can't deal with what's to come. It's unknown.

When you're riding a horse, you can only jump the hurdle in front of you. You can't jump the hurdle that's in the next field, or which might be there tomorrow.

The passage in Matthew that we are reading today is so important. It talks about looking at God first, before all else – which I believe is the key to well-being and peace. Looking to God, walking in a way that pleases him *now*, developing that relationship with him *today*, and our closeness with him, brings a greater sense of his presence and assurance.

Having said that, although we shouldn't worry about tomorrow, it's not always wrong to make provision for ourselves if we are able to do so. Genesis 41 tells the story of the beleaguered Joseph, who rose to a position of prominence in Egypt, acted wisely during famine, and so was able to provide for many, many people.

But we're not always in a position to be able to save, to provide, for our own tomorrows. We can be living in a beautiful house but circumstances change and we lose everything. When I was involved in street evangelism, I met people living in shop doorways who had held professional positions till something happened that they couldn't deal with. Conversely, we can be unemployed, then find a wonderful job; one phone call can change the course of our lives. That happened to me: one call, offering me work from home when I was suffering from agoraphobia, and my world opened up with new opportunities.

We simply don't know what's round the corner.

Today is the day we are living in.

Let's make good decisions to put God first, and to do what pleases him. Let's live *now* and trust him with tomorrow.

Reflection

- What are you thankful for, right now?
- What's the hurdle in front of you?
- What one thing do you need to ask God for, today?

Stand by for action!

Either find a picture of a tree on the internet, or look at one for real. Draw it, paint it, write about what you see – or simply observe it.

If it's possible, depending on the season, look at a tree with no leaves on the branches.

It's alive, but it looks dead.

Its shape is obvious during the winter season; it is hidden by leaves in the summer.

Imagine the tree swaying in the breeze. The wind picks up – what does the tree do?

Things that are alive can look dead, where they might just be dormant for a season.

When the leaves are off the tree, nothing is hidden. God sees us with the 'leaves off', if you like.

The circumstances of life can bend and shape us, or they can break us.

Journal any thoughts, and review them again later.

Conclusion

In John 3, Jesus spoke of the Holy Spirit – like the wind, blowing 'wherever it pleases' (v. 8).

Fear can make us rigid. If we truly want to seek God and his righteousness, we need to be able to surrender to the wind of his Spirit, to relax and trust him, and to move and sway with him as we move through the seasons of our lives.

Lord, thank you that I am here today, alive, and able to know you. Help me to surrender to you, so that I can feel your joy and your presence right now, knowing tomorrow belongs to you. Amen.

5

Revelation 22:1-5a

Then the angel showed me the river of the water of life, as clear as crystal, flowing from the throne of God and of the Lamb down the middle of the great street of the city. … No longer will there be any curse. The throne of God and of the Lamb will be in the city … They will see his face, and his name will be on their foreheads. There will be no more night.

I live halfway up a hill, overlooking the town, so the view from the window of my spare room is breath-taking. At night-time, I sometimes stand there and pray. The night holds an awesomeness, a sense of eternity as I look at the myriad specks of light, some in people's houses, but some twinkling in the sky, put there by God.

I used to really enjoy night-times, when I was younger. For me, the night was a time of excitement – dancing, meeting friends. But it can also be lonely and frightening.

When my mum was living at home, she would have seizures in the middle of the night. She had a big old creaky bed, so when I heard it making a noise, I knew there was trouble.

One night, I heard creaking, felt woozy because I'd got up so fast, opened my bedroom door, hit my head on the side of it, knocked myself out and fell on my face, breaking my nose. To this day I have a two-inch scar on my forehead.

We're promised, if we know Jesus, that in the future there 'will be no more night'.

No more night? No more admiring the stars, or parties and dancing?

I don't think that this means there'll be an absence of wonder and awe, or friendship and fun. But it will mean a permanent end to the darkness that so often snaps at our heels, and manifests as fear, anxiety and other negative emotions. How will we be able to feel any of those things, living face-to-face with a God who loves us, and welcomes us fully into his eternal presence?

Of course, we can know his presence now, but on this earth, it is as if 'we see through a glass, darkly' (1 Corinthians 13:12, KJV).

'In this world you will have trouble', says Jesus. 'But take heart! I have overcome the world' (John 16:33). If he has 'overcome the world', he has overcome our situation. Nothing is impossible for him (Mark 10:27).

He died on the cross to pay the price of separation from ourselves and God. He was raised from death to ratify what he had done – it's all true: he is who he says he is, and all his promises are therefore reliable.

We can trust him. He loves us. We are saved by his free favour, not by any act of striving (Ephesians 2:8-9). It's a gift, as much as a birthday present held out to us by a loving friend.

Let's remember that God invites us to rest in him, and to do everything from that position of rest. He accomplished everything we need for salvation, and life, on the cross. We don't have to prove ourselves. We don't have to add anything. It's not Jesus' work on the cross *and...* my good works/me being perfect/my observing religious rituals...

He invites us into the freedom he has already bought for us. He has clothed us with his righteousness. We don't have any of our own. 1 Corinthians 1:30 says: '... you are in Christ Jesus, who has become for us wisdom from God – that is, our righteousness, holiness and redemption.' That's right. He *himself* is our wisdom, righteousness, holiness and redemption!

That very thought should still our hearts and give us peace.

And as we walk in his freedom, his peace, his love, it should leak out, like a colander, to the person in front of us: the person who really needs to know that there is a God, there is good news, and he loves them – right now, today.

Reflection

- Whatever the 'night' represents for you, remember that it won't last forever.
- What does it mean for you that Jesus has 'overcome the world'?
- 'Here's my gift to you,' says Jesus. 'My own righteousness and holiness.' How does that change your perspective on 'works'?

Stand by for action!

Remember the labyrinth from Week 1? Look at it now. If you didn't do this, and drew a timeline of your life instead, look at that.

If you have illustrated your labyrinth, what could you add at this point?

Or what could you add to your timeline?

How, through reading this book, have you drawn closer to God? In what ways have you been challenged? Or encouraged?

Conclusion

When I was ill, one time, I was lying on the floor unable to move. My mother had called the doctor, but she said something to me that I have never forgotten: 'All things pass.' God may not immediately change tricky circumstances, but if we can draw nearer to him, then our perspective on our problems and the issues of life may change. And we can be assured of a future where the troubles of this life will be gone forever. Romans 13:12 tells us, 'The night is nearly over; the day is almost here.' How many people in your own life need to hear that good news?

> *Jesus, thank you that you are Lord and God. Thank you that you invite us to share your life and eternity. Help me today to know who it is you'd like me to speak to, come alongside, share with or pray for, so that they might know you better too. Amen.*

Weekend exercise

Think of the 'I am' statements of Jesus, declaring who he was. These can be found in John 6:35; 8:12; 10:7-9; 10:14-15; 11:25-26; 14:6; 15:1-4.

If you don't have time to read them all, pick just one and meditate on it over the weekend. Draw all you can from the words. For example, if you have chosen 'I am the resurrection and the life' (John 11:25), reflect on verse 26, where Jesus asks 'Do you believe this?', and imagine him asking that of you.

In Revelation 1:18 we read: 'I am the Living One; I was dead, and now look, I am alive for ever and ever! And I hold the keys of death and Hades.'

How might a fresh revelation of who Jesus is enable us to trust him more?

Jesus is the 'I am' – this is the name by which God revealed himself to Moses (Exodus 3:14). God exists eternally, but it is in the 'now' that we can experience him. So often we don't take time to be in the present moment, where God dwells, and hear from him, or enjoy his presence.

We don't always have to be striving, seeking, cajoling, pleading, working, doing.

Sometimes we need to simply... stop. Rest!

Write a prayer. It might be long, or it could be short. If you don't want to write anything down, find a peaceful place, and just 'be with him'.

At the start of this book, I asked if you had a journey with God, and to think about where he had come through for you, in the past. Can you write something on the page if you left it blank?

Blank pages in life are OK. But better to fill them with a testimony of what *God* can do, than to let fear write all over them.

Last Word

At the beginning of our journey together, I mentioned that I used to live in a cinema. Weird, I know. I can still remember the doors clattering when people hared off into the night when the movie had finished, rushing off to lives I'd never know.

So much of life is a mystery. Mysteries can be fun, or they can be scary. Sometimes they are resolved, sometimes not.

In the movie of life, there can often be more questions than answers, uncertainties, loose ends that aren't always neatly wrapped up. There are silences – blank pages. But silence isn't always something to be afraid of. It is in the silence, the quiet, in the times of rest that we often hear more clearly from the One who never leaves us. He may not always give us the answer we are looking for, but he does give us himself.

As for 'the void'… well, as an adult, I think I'd have flicked on a light and seen it for what it was. Just a big empty space that actually did serve some purpose, as access to the roof. It wasn't a room I'd choose to spend time in, with others or alone. But in the light of day, and adulthood, it was nothing to actually be afraid of.

It was only years later that I realised that that the scary, silent, broken space didn't exist anymore. The cinema we'd lived in had been demolished, and along with it, 'the void' – which was now only a memory.

In a sense, that's a picture of what happens when we come to Christ. 2 Corinthians 5:17 tells us: 'Therefore, if anyone is in Christ, the new creation has come: the old has gone, the new is here!' Fears that rise up, the big, scary emptiness that makes no sense and haunts our dreams and imaginings, the dread that wraps itself around our hearts… let's remember that the old 'room' they inhabited has gone. That old building has been demolished. Their whispers are echoes of who we were before we met the One who sets us free. Jesus has better rooms for us to live in (John 14:2). He's already preparing them for us. Heaven awaits – when we really will know the abundance of new life (John 10:10) that we get a glimpse of here.

And if Jesus already is preparing somewhere for you and for me, then we needn't fear he'd ever leave us while we're journeying through this often perplexing world. 'Come near to me,' he says, 'and I'll come near to you' (see James 4:8). What a great invitation – for us, and for those we hope to share our freedom with! We can rest in him, trusting that he has accomplished everything we need to be able to live the 'God life'.

I hope you are able to come away from this book with a fresh understanding that once we begin to follow Jesus, we're in a two-way relationship with a much stronger 'Other'. He is the 'Prince of Peace' (Isaiah 9:6). So, coming to him is to come to the very stillness we need.

We're known.

We're loved.

We're accepted.

Rest in him!

Helpful Books

Clare Blake and Chris Ledger, *Insight into Anxiety* (Surrey: CWR, 2011)

Graham Dow (ed), *Pathways to Prayer* (London: DLT, 1996)

Brother Lawrence, *The Practice of the Presence of God* (New Kensington, PA: Whitaker House, 1982)

Watchman Nee, *Sit, Walk, Stand* (Eastbourne: Kingsway, 1994)